Tales of Old Cambridgeshire

Other counties in this series include:

Avon	Lincolnshire
Berkshire	Northamptonshire
Buckinghamshire	Oxfordshire
Dorset	Somerset
East Anglia	Stratford
Essex	Suffolk
Gloucestershire	Surrey
Hampshire	Sussex
Herefordshire	Warwickshire
Hertfordshire	Wiltshire
Kent	Worcestershire

Tales of Old Cambridgeshire

Polly Howat

With Illustrations by Don Osmond

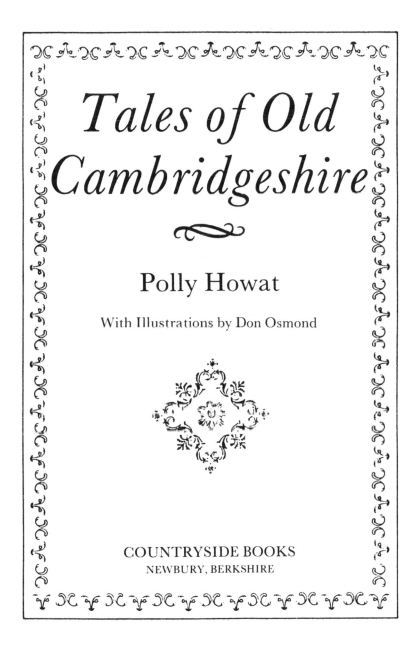

COUNTRYSIDE BOOKS
NEWBURY, BERKSHIRE

First Published 1990
© Polly Howat 1990
Reprinted 1999, 2004

COUNTRYSIDE BOOKS
3 CATHERINE ROAD
NEWBURY, BERKSHIRE

ISBN 1 85306 086 0

Cover painting from an original
by Colin Doggett

Produced through MRM Associates Ltd., Reading
Typeset by Acorn Bookwork, Salisbury
Printed in England by J. W. Arrowsmith Ltd., Bristol

To my husband
and children, with love.

To Hannah
Best Wishes
Bmy Hart
2013

Acknowledgements

I am grateful to the Cambridgeshire Collection, Cambridgeshire Library for permission to use their illustrative material and to the curator of the Wisbech and Fenland Museum for similar consent.

Thanks are also given to the curator of the Cambridge Folk Museum for allowing me to use notes from Edith Porter's unpublished work regarding the Burwell Alphabet and the tale of William the Reeve's son.

Contents

CONTENTS

CAMBRIDGESHIRE — The map overleaf is by John Speede and shows the county as it was in the early seventeenth century.

CAMBRIDGE

The armes of R. Sigebert founder of the Vniuersity

St Peters House 1280.

Pembroke Hall 1343.

Trinitie Hall 1347.

Kings Colledge 1441.

St Katherins Hall 1475.

Christs Colledge 1505.

Magdalen Colledge 1519.

Chrisk places in the Citie observed by Alphabeticall letters.
A. Trinitye Colledge.
B. Kinges Colledge.
C. Clare Hall.
D. Caius Colledge.
E. Saint Iohns Colledge.
F. Saint Sepulchre.
G. All hollowes in S. Iury
H. Saint Michael.
I. Trinitye Church.
K. Saint Edward.
L. Saint Benets.
M. Corpus Christi Coll:
N. Saint Peters.
O. Saint Gyles.
P. Magdalen Colledge.
Q. Christes Colledge.
R. Saint Andrew.
S. Iesus Colledge.
V. Quenes Colledge.
W. Saint Botolphe.
X. Pembrok Hall.
Y. Peter house.
Z. Saint Clement.
1. Litle Saint Maries.
2. The Castle.

WEST

Pembrok Hall Orchard.
S. Thomas lus.

N

PART OF LINCOLN SHIRE

Spalding
Coubet
Crowland
Dowsdale
WISBICH
Thorney
Eldernall
Whittlesey
Whittlesey Dike
Whittlesey Mere

GIRVII. or We

THE ILE OF

Yaxley
Tykeworth
Stilton
Holme
Cunnyngton

PART OF HVNTING-TON SHIRE

Ramsey
Bury
Wistow
Sutton
Somersham
Bluntsham
Woodhurst
Huntingdon
S. Ives
Godmanchester
Hemingford
Offordes
Begars bushe
Toseland
Wintering-ham
S. Neot
Graueley
Papworth anuies
Papworth euered
Elsworth
Boxworth
Groxton
Caxton
Kitapwell
Madinley
Childresley
Hardwick

PAFWORTH

HV:

STOW

Warsley Tetworth
Gransden Buries
Stow
Kingston
Gransden pua
Gamlingay
Potton
Hatley S. George
Cokinghatley
Tadlow
Biglesware
Dunton
Hennworth

PARTE OF BEDFORD SHIRE

Wimple
Haslingfeld
Arrington. Walton
Crawden
Clopton
Wendie
Steple morden
Abbington
Steple
Lytlington

WETHERLEE
Eucksen
Eucksenkm ma
HV:
Oxmel
HVa
Wenbo
Surueys
ARNINGFORD
Bassmeme
Ne

HVN:

PARE HARTFORD

S

Performed by IOHN SPEEDE And are to be solde in popes head alley, by John Sudbury and G. Humbell.
ANNo.

EMANVL
Emanuel Colledge 1584.

William brother to Ranulph E. of Chester

Iohn of Renaud vncle to Phillip R. to Edward I.

William Marques of Iuliers

Edm Du

PART OF NOR: FOLK.

DIEV ET MON DROIT

CAMBRIDGSHIRE described with
the deuision of the hundreds, the
Townes situation, with the Armes of
the Colleges of that famous Vniuersiti:

And also the Armes
of all such Princes and
noble-men as haue heer:
tofore borne the honor:
able tytles & dignities of
the Earldome of Cambridg.

PART OF SVFFOLKE

PARTE OF ESSEX

Cum Priuilegio.
1610.

The Armes of the
Vniuersitie

Clare Hall
1326.

Corpus Christi
Colledge. 1344.

Gonuile & Caius
College. 1348.

Queenes Colledge
1448.

Iesus Colledge
1502.

St Iohns Colledge
1508.

Trinitie Colledge.
1546.

Edward Duke
of York.

Richard Earle
of Cambridge.

Richard Duke
of York.

The
Great
Skating Race

SKATING has been in the blood of born and bred Cambridgeshire folk since the days when the old 'Fen Slodgers' walked about on stilts and slid on the ice with skates made from animal bones. It is thought that the Dutch drainers brought their metal skates with long upturned ends with them when they came to work in our lowlands in the 17th century. The 'Fen Runners' beloved of so many skaters well into this century are of a similar design.

In past times when winters offered weeks of frozen weather some really splendid sport and entertainment was available. Throughout the county skating contests were arranged with local farmers providing the prizes, which included such welcome things as fat pigs, pieces of beef, purses of money, flannel petticoats, bonnets and fancy gloves. Contestants and spectators could buy warming gin, hot potatoes and roasted chestnuts from the vendors who set up their stalls on the ice.

The contests took place on a half mile course with a barrel marker at each end and with sides of banked snow. Each race was over two miles and the committee selected 16 entrants who were paired, usually by lot, and ran against each other in eight races for the first heat. The eight winners were paired for the next heat and so on until the victor emerged. Between

1879 and 1956 19 professional Championships of Great Britain were held with venues at Thorney, Swavesey, Lingay Fen, Littleport, Bury Fen, Milton and Crowland on the Lincolnshire border.

The northern area produced many champions; a few names brought to mind include the Drakes from Chatteris, Egars from Thorney, Larmen Register from Southery (Norfolk border) and the great Welney men, 'Turkey' Smart, his nephew 'Flying Fish' and the amazing William 'Gutta Percha' See, so called because just like the gutta percha rubber used for soling shoes, he was equally tough and strong!

One of the best of the skating stories is the tale of the time when Larmen Register raced the 12.30 pm train from Littleport to Ely in 1875.

It all began when a group of Ely men were waiting in the refreshment room at Cambridge station for their train to take them back home. An official from the Great Eastern Railway Company was within earshot and bragging about this new method of transport which had spread throughout the region. Being 'good ol' boys' the Ely men chipped in that the trains from Ely were so slow, why, you could skate faster than one of those new contraptions could chug along! The weather was severe at the time of the meeting and a wager was set that a man would be found to take on the train from Sandhill Bridge at Littleport down to Ely railway bridge.

The Great Eastern Railway official guaranteed that the driver of the train would be completely unaware that the race was taking place, the men laid their bets and took the slow train back to Ely. Larmen Register, the great racing man from Southery on the Norfolk border, agreed to be their man and like all good secrets it soon leaked out and produced a full purse. The railway company did not keep to its bargain, announcing on the appointed day that the 12.30 pm train from Littleport would race the skater along the four mile stretch of line which ran parallel with the river Ouse.

Larmen Register was in fine form as he waited with his

pacer for the 12.30 to blow its whistle at Sandhill Bridge and they sped off, their streamlined bodies cutting into the freezing early afternoon. The high bank prevented them from seeing the train but they kept their ears strained for the dreaded chug of the panting competitor. The pacer was succeeded by another, but he too dropped out before they reached Adelaide Bridge. Neither man nor engine faltered, their resolute breath sending similar patterns into the freezing air, each having a reputation to maintain.

Just as Register was coming up to the bridge he noticed a pile of cinders and clinker had been strewn across his path. He slowed down and picked his way through the mess, his anger giving him extra impetus to complete the race. He flashed off and reached Ely Bridge half a minute before his opponent.

The victor and his backers were outraged by the cinder trick and vowed to get even with the railway company, who denied all knowledge of the vandalism. Rather foolishly they insisted that the men refrain from taking any action that night as HRH the Prince of Wales would be travelling on the 7.30 train on his way to Sandringham. The men agreed to hold back but only if they were permitted to travel in the carriage next to the Prince. Reluctantly the officials agreed to their demands and the men set off in a happy mood to the Lamb Hotel to make plans.

As dusk fell that evening any person with sharp eyes would have seen a handful of men skating down the Ouse carrying unlit red lanterns. The 7.30 train drew in at Ely station and the avengers piled into their allotted carriage, their eyes bright with anticipation of what was to follow.

One mile out of Ely the driver was halted by a red light shining down the track. His porter set off to make his abortive investigation, and after a long wait the train steamed off. A little while later another red light shone in his track and the tedious wait started once more. At each stop the men threw down their window so they could lean out and enjoy the spectacle. On the fourth stop the Prince of Wales also poked his head out of his window and bellowed out 'Is this blasted train ever going to get me to Sandringham this night?'

Jimmy, William and Tansley Luddington, Arthur and Bertram Hall and the mighty Larmen Register had got even with the Great Eastern Railway Company. The company was left with egg on its face, having incurred the displeasure of the Prince of Wales. Quite probably the event was mulled over many a pint of beer, the day that Larmen beat the 12.30 pm train to Ely!

The Upware Bustle

COPROLITE is fossilised animal excrement in the form of phosphate nodules, known locally as 'bear's dung', which was found in the greensand levels of much of south-west and east Cambridgeshire. Although it had been suggested at a meeting of the British Association held in Cambridge in 1845 that such a stratum covered many square miles of the county near to the surface, nothing was done until after the discovery made by a Burwell miller, John Ball, in 1851.

Ball dug up some coprolites which were close to the surface of his land. He washed the mud from these hard round nodules which were then ground down in his mill. After some experimentation he mixed in the right amount of sulphuric acid and, after a few more days and further processing, made excellent artificial manure. He later quit flour milling and concentrated upon processing and selling coprolite.

It was not until the early 1860s that the industry boomed into life and produced such a fever of activity that it became compared with an American gold rush. The districts of the greatest activity embraced the villages of Soham, Burwell, Swaffham, Horningsea, Grantchester, Barrington, Reach, Upware, Abington Piggots, Wendy, Whaddon, Bassingbourn and Barnwell, to name but a few. The owners of land on which deposits were found were quick to lease it to prospectors, usually for a three year period, which in its heyday could command up to £150 per acre. Despite this high price profit

15

returns were good, for one acre could yield some 300 tons of phosphate at £2.10s a ton. Despite the clause which stipulated that the mined land should be returned to the owner in the same condition as when it was first leased, the top and sub soils were often jumbled up with the gault level, which resulted in heavy land and subsequent poor crop yield.

The phosphate trade took off so quickly that quiet agricultural villages were turned almost overnight into busy industrial communities, with a large influx of workers anxious to benefit from the good wages which came with this sometimes dangerous new work. The diggers worked at piece rates which ranged from between 1½d to 4½d per cubic yard. A hardworking man could easily earn from 18 shillings to £1 a week compared with land wages of some eleven shillings a week. The drift from fields to open cast coprolite mines was so great that farmers increased their rate of pay to £1 a week but still the men preferred the new challenge.

The work was always over-shadowed by danger. The large number of injuries and fatalities prompted the Secretary of Addenbrooke's Hospital, Cambridge to write to the *Cambridge Chronicle* dated 1st June 1875, on behalf of the hospital's governors who deplored the number of needless accidents and hoped the letter would prompt better safety regulations and methods of extraction.

Excavation was done by hand and involved digging a trench which was then undermined and the coprolite shovelled out. 'Watchmen' were supposed to stand at the top of the excavation to watch for any sign of the earth breaking away as the men dug in. However, they were not always provided, or did not remain on duty for the whole of the digging.

As the trenches were exhausted they were filled in and apart from a ribbed pattern in some fields there is little trace of this industry, which at the time caused such an upheaval on the landscape. Plenty of water was needed for washing the nodules and if natural supplies were unavailable streams were dammed or huge ponds dug, which in time provided a good natural habitat for wildlife. The cleaned coprolite was then carted off to the processing mills, often by lightercraft if there was easy access to a waterway. If not the new railways offered very competitive rates and greater speed, and road networks were built for the trade.

The sudden influx of so many working men into small close-knit communities often changed the accustomed rhythm of their social traditions. Take for instance what happened in Upware in 1862, which was known as the 'Upware Bustle'.

The village was part of a major coprolite mining area where at Rogationtide its neighbours enjoyed a fair and a festival. The miners thought they should have a 'Bustle' in upware on one of the Rogation Days and duly arranged for the setting up of all the trappings of a good day's fun, which included dancing-booths, skittle alleys and shellfish stalls. Many of the houses hung green boughs from their windows as it was customary for the licensing authorities to allow any such house to sell alcohol during Rogation. 'Bough-houses' were a tradition in many parts of England during the time of their particular fair or festival.

It was reported that between 10 am and 11 am the event began to get out of hand when boxing turned into free-fighting, most probably fuelled by countless trips to the bough-houses. The police were quickly drafted from nearby Wicken, but the coprolite diggers soon gave them a soaking in the nearby Fen drain and the police returned to their own base and were not seen for the rest of the 'Bustle'.

The fighting was said to have been egged on by the 'King of Upware', alias Richard Ramsey Fielder, MA, graduate of Jesus College, Cambridge and a member of Lincolns Inn, who had taken up residence in the equally eccentric sounding inn, the 'Five Miles from Anywhere – No Hurry' in the early 1860s. This inn was the headquarters of an exclusive Cambridge students club known as the 'Upware Republic' which they ran as a sham country with its own president.

Fielder has been described as a crank, who always carried a

17

big earthenware jug known as 'His Majesty's Pint' which was filled with rum punch, and like the lightermen with whom he spent most of his time quarrelling, he too wore a waistcoat of scarlet. When the river trade declined and he had no further source of argument he took up his pint jug and retired to Folkestone!

Therefore this 'Bustle' had two potential sources of disorder, the coprolite diggers and 'King Fielder'. An eyewitness account stated that:

'Shoals of people were everywhere about, the heat was intense, the dancing-booths were crammed full, pugilism was in the air, fighting was going on in all directions, in close proximity to love-making; many of the crowd were lying on the grass overcome with the heat or more likely with having taken too much "nourishment", and there was a babble of noise from the harp and violins, the blowing of horns, and concertina playing. . .' As night fell the revellers returned home, some so drunk they fell into the waterway!

Eventually the fertiliser boom ended as quickly as it started, except for a brief revival at some mines during the First World War when the phosphate was sent off to the Midlands factories to be turned into munitions. Its downfall was the discovery in America of huge tracts of coprolite which lay very close to the surface. The Cambridgeshire producers could not begin to compete with the low priced foreign imports which came flooding into this country. Diggings were soon abandoned, fortunes lost and hundreds of men left without work. One company went on to become a present household word — Fisons Agrochemicals — which is one of the largest fertiliser companies in this country and was founded by the brothers Joseph and Samuel Fison, who between them leased and worked coprolite mines at Stow-cum-Quy, Haslingfield, Horningsea and Shelford.

18

But many villages were left with legacies of heavy land, reed-fringed ponds and empty public houses as reminders of a brief time when agriculture gave way to the industrial pursuit of 'bear's dung' and fortunes were made and lost almost overnight.

The Gorefield Poltergeist

J OE Scrimshaw, or 'Skrimmie' as the locals called him, was a
wealthy Gorefield farmer with a bluff nature and fond-
ness for beer. He lived at North View, a small farmhouse
which was built in 1909 on the old Turnover Bank, together
with his mother and daughter Olive, who was a gentle,
sensitive girl aged 14 years. Little did the Scrimshaws realise
when they awoke on the 12th February, 1923 that before
nightfall their lives would be changed forever.

Everything was quite normal until the afternoon turned to
dusk. As usual Granny Scrimshaw went to light the oil lamps
and make everthing cosy for Joe's return home, but no
matter what she did the lamps refused to light. Olive was sent
out to the kitchen to find the candles, which remained as dark
as the lamps. Joe came into the gloomy house and he too failed
to lighten the place. And then, quite suddenly, there in the
half light of the sitting room the pianola which must have
weighed several hundredweight simply tipped over and lay in
a jangling heap. One by one pictures fell from their hooks, the
clock crashed into the fire hearth and the ornaments danced
off the mantelpiece. The heavy dining table moved about the
room and Joe's cherished barometer joined the rest of the
debris on the linoleum. The Scrimshaws were terrified out of
their wits, too alarmed to move.

They were brought back to life by the now all too familiar sound coming from the kitchen. Fearing for the safety of their everyday china and Sunday-best services they quickly placed their valuables on the big scrubbed-top kitchen table, believing them to be safer there than hanging on hooks and balanced on plate racks. Everything was eerily quiet as they went about their task and locked the kitchen door behind them. For a time all seemed calm, but then, after an hour or more, there was one huge crash from behind the secured door and all their chinaware was broken to smithereens — and this word is chosen with care. Not one thing was just cracked or broken in two. Everything was in tiny pieces as if some terrible force had crashed down upon the table, which remained unharmed.

Neighbours were called in to witness the mayhem and they walked with caution amongst the rubble of Joe's possessions, for the lamps still refused to light. Quiet eventually returned to this terrified Fen house, the lamps flickered into life and with great trepidation the family went to bed. This was the cue for washstands and dressing tables to dance around the bedrooms, and window blinds to shoot up and down. Peace was not restored until dawn.

The very next morning Olive was sent to stay with relatives and she never returned to that troubled house. After the girl's departure the police were called in and they too witnessed scenes which they told the press 'could have no mortal origin.' The disturbances continued sporadically until the 16th February when they abated for a few days.

It was assumed that a poltergeist was responsible for Skrimmie's troubles and the local newspapers had a field day and gave the 'Haunted House' a lot of coverage. This was picked up by the national press who sent their reporters down for eyewitness accounts. Joe met them outside his house and told them it was 'A brute' and complained that hordes of sightseers were trying to get into his house and were stealing bits from the huge pile of china debris which lay in his front garden.

THE GOREFIELD POLTERGEIST

The press had just missed a coachload of people who had travelled from Long Sutton!

Soon letters of advice were being sent from all over the country, some from obvious cranks and others offering sensible advice. They received one from Sir Arthur Conan Doyle, addressed from the Victoria and Albert Hotel, Torquay which was verified by the press as being genuine. Sir Arthur wrote: 'As I have made a study of such cases, I will advise you what to do. You should send your daughter away for a rest and change. Then open all your windows, ventilate well, and you will find the phenomena after a day or so cease altogether.

'It is not that your daughter plays any conscious part in this, but it is that at certain times some persons throw out an atmosphere or vapour which can be used in a material way by intelligent forces outside ourselves. These forces break and move material objects. They can best be described as mischievous material children of the psychic world. The 'medium' who throws out this atmosphere is nearly always a child from 10 to 16 and generally a girl.'

This is an interesting letter as there is now a growing belief that noisy spirits or poltergeists tend to be found in areas of frustration and unhappiness, most often in the vicinity of adolescents and occasionally of elderly people. Not long before the 'poltergeisting', Mrs Scrimshaw had left the matrimonial home taking her other child with her and leaving Olive with Joe. This was an obviously distressing time for the young girl. Could her extreme unhappiness have manifested sufficient supernatural energy to cause the poltergeist? The troubles persisted for some while after she had left the house.

Advice was sought from the local vicar, the Reverend J. Hagley Rutter, who did not express too much concern and remained non-committal. However a farmer from neighbouring Wisbech St Mary came up with a bright idea. Was it really a poltergeist or ghost that was terrorising Skrimmie, or was it witchcraft? Perhaps Joe had had the 'evil-eye' put on him by someone who wanted revenge? The same thing had happened to him some years before, the farmer said, when all his stock had suddenly died in mysterious circumstances. He had got help from the local wise-woman, Mrs Harriet Holmes, a smallholder from Chalk Road, Leverington, whom he said possessed remarkable powers and had removed the cause of his misery.

The *News of the World* is believed to have paid for her services and she was duly summoned to the stricken house where she performed her ritual spell-breaking with a small medicine bottle filled with a number of black-headed apple pips, some pins, a paring from Joe's fingernail and pieces of hair taken from Granny Scrimshaw and Olive. The bottle was well stoppered and then placed in the kitchen fire. She locked the Scrimshaws outside, telling them that when the bottle burst from the heat of the fire, their troubles would burst with it.

Did Mrs Holmes cast off a spell? She certainly used a commonplace form of anti-hexing by making a link between the Scrimshaws and the 'magic', in this case hair, nail clippings and apple pips, for Joe was a fruit farmer. The pins were intended to prick and release the malevolence, which surely enough appeared to flee from the farmhouse on Turnover Bank.

Or was 'it' more clever than she was; for on 5th March 1923, Harriet Mary Holmes, aged 59, who was in good health and knew the area blindfolded, was found face down outside her house, drowned in some six inches of dyke water. Later calculations determined that at about the time of her death the poltergeist had returned for a short time to cause more mischief and then it went away, but not forever. Over the ensuing years residents of North View claim to have encountered the supernatural and on occasions the present tenants hear the uncanny sounds of breaking crockery.

The Royal Recluse

IN the Quaker burial ground at Wisbech is the grave of one Jane Stuart, who died on 12th July 1742, aged 88 years. Her grave is easily recognised by her initials and year of death laid out with box hedging. Attached to it there is an interesting, but rather sad tale.

Jane Stuart, born 1654, was reputed to be the natural daughter of James II and half-sister to Queen Mary and Queen Anne. Her mother is unknown but was said to be a Protestant. Jane became a staunch member of the Quaker movement and was persecuted for her beliefs.

Just before her wedding day her fiance was killed in a tragic accident when the coach in which they were travelling overturned. Jane Stuart was physically unhurt, but mentally shattered, her life rendered empty apart from her religion. A few days after the burial she put on a heavy disguise and secretly left London. She fled to Wisbech, where she found cheap lodgings in the miserable cellar of a house in the Old Market, close to Oil Mill Lane.

Alexander Peckover, from the prominent Quaker and banking family who lived in what is now called Peckover House, a National Trust property on the North Brink, made some notes in the 19th century concerning this reclusive girl, who had been known to friends of his family.

Apparently her arrival in the Fenland town coincided with harvest time and she joined the rest of the farm labourers who offered themselves for employment from the Town Bridge. A farmer asked if she could reap. Jane replied that although she had never tried she would do her best. By nightfall she was so accomplished she was called the 'Queen of the Reapers', although no-one equated the given royal title with her true identity, which she always took great pains to conceal.

Although a regular attender at the Friends Meeting House on the North Brink, she lived a reclusive life and scratched a meagre living from spinning worsted in her dull room, which she sold from a market stall. It was on such an occasion that she recognised the coach belonging to the Duke of Argyll when it drew up at the Rose and Crown Inn. Jane quickly went back to her lodgings as the Duke enquired as to the whereabouts of this Royal offspring. Heads were shaken, for nobody could tell that this strange quiet girl from the Old Market was the woman they sought.

This humble, kind hearted girl was well liked by those few people who knew her. She liked to talk to her caged birds who shared her underground room, for when the curtains were drawn and the lamp lit she opened their doors and they flew unhindered about the place.

On one occasion she was walking in the graveyard at the back of the Meeting House when she fell to the ground in a fainting fit. She later asked that a tree be planted to mark the place. Her request was carried out but, according to Mr Peckover, the tree in time grew too large and was dug up and sold for twelve shillings. It was replaced with box hedging clipped into the legend 'JS AGED 88'. Sadly the years have taken their toll but there are plans to replace it with cuttings taken from the original stock.

This is all we know of this shy Royal girl who worked hard but lived in poverty in a dank room, who could read the New Testament in Greek but was only at ease with her pet birds.

The Tale
of
Tom Hickathrift

THE legendary giant Tom Hickathrift was supposed to have lived near Wisbech in the Isle of Ely, around the time of William the Conqueror. His story probably first appeared in print in 1790 when *The History of Tom Hickathrift* was written by Boston and published in a small pamphlet known as a chapbook, which cost one penny. Chapbooks were hawked in the streets by chapmen and certainly this version was not intended for children as it contains a couple of rather rude phrases! The giant's tale was however later written for children, both in chapbook and conventional form. One of the best versions can be found in J. Orchard Halliwell's *Popular Rhymes and Nursery Tales*, which was first published in 1849. Halliwell was a great authority on children's rhymes and tales and carried out extensive research into the subject, his main source being the oral tradition.

Unfortunately the story of Hickathrift is not known by many people living in the Wisbech area but his memory has been preserved by the villages of Marshland St James and Tilney All Saints in Norfolk, who have incorporated his effigy into their attractive wooden village signs. Tom's fine house and estate were said to be in the former village and his body lies in the churchyard of the latter.

There is not room for the whole of Hickathrift's story in this instance, but a shortened version is appropriate with quotes from Boston's chapbook. A fuller story can be read in Enid Porter's *Cambridgeshire Customs and Folklore*.

In this instance the story is set in Saxon times. He was a lazy boy, and 'At ten years he was six feet high and three feet in thickness, his hand was like a shoulder of mutton and every other part proportionable, but his strength was yet unknown.' When fully grown he measured some eight ft and surprised his neighbours when he carried over '2,000 weight' of straw home on his back from a farmer's field, so that his mother could refill her straw mattresses.

He began work for a King's Lynn brewer, bringing the beer from Lynn to Wisbech and across the marshes. This involved a journey of some 20 miles, which could have been considerably shortened if he could have cut across the Smeeth, a desolate wasteland, which was guarded by a terrible giant who killed all trespassers. In the end laziness made him take the crossing and he was immediately confronted by his adversary who ran off to his cave to fetch his club. Tom's brains were in danger of being clubbed from his head, but although unarmed he was truly innovative. He quickly turned his cart over, removed a wheel for his shield and the axle-tree, the rod connecting the wheels, for his sword. Soon the wicked giant lay dead at our hero's feet and his large treasure hoard was in Tom's cart. There was great rejoicing when his neighbours heard the news, 'And bonfires made all round the country for Tom's success.'

The giant's cave was replaced by Tom with a fine house in which he and widow Hickathrift lived, with part of the giant's land forming their estate. The remainder of the land he gave to the poor for their common and close to his house he built a church which he dedicated to St James. It was on that saint's day that he had killed the terror of the Smeeth.

Marshland St James is a village within the parish of Emneth, West Norfolk and its present church, which has the same dedication, was built in 1896. A large part of the village is known as the Smeeth, it also has Hickathrift Crossroads, Hickathrift House and Farm and in between the two lay Hickathrift's Washbasin, which was a large indentation in the field which now has new housing stock. His 'Candlestick' or 'Collar Stud' stood close by until a few years ago when it vanished. However, two similar stones known as 'Hickathrift's Candlesticks', which could be the remains of ancient stone crosses, still stand in Tilney All Saints and Terrington St John graveyards. The giant is reputed to be buried under three unmarked slabs of stone which together measure 8ft and lie against the footpath on the eastern side of Tilney All Saints graveyard.

By now Tom was known as 'Mr Thomas Hickathrift' and reached another landmark when he met a tinker, Henry Nonsuch, who was looking for the man who slew the Smeeth giant, for he wished to match his own strength against this man. The tinker was almost as large as Tom and after a long battle Nonsuch emerged the victor. They shook hands, became firm friends and together righted many wrongs.

Their following adventure is interesting. They were dispatched to Ely by the sheriff to quell a great uprising involving some 10,000 people 'who contended for their rights and privileges which they said had been greatly infringed.' If we take the tale to be set after the Norman invasion this would have been the insurrections which took place in that part of the Isle of Ely between 1066–1071 when the Saxons led by Hereward the Wake held out against the Norman soldiers. True to nursery tale form, our two friends won the day. The king rewarded them by bestowing a knighthood upon Tom and settling 40 shillings a year on the tinker.

Sir Thomas went on to wed a beautiful, young rich widow from Cambridge, having first fought off her other suitors. After their wedding they were invited to court, at which time the king heard of a wicked giant who was terrorising the Isle of Thanet in Kent. This miscreant had only one eye which was placed in the middle of his forehead, and had hair 'the texture

30

of rusty wire' which hung down like coils of snakes. This fairy tale monstrosity rode on a miserable dragon, accompanied by a troupe of lions and bears. Soon all their heads had been cut off by the king's humble servant from Cambridgeshire and his reward this time was to be made Governor of the Isle of Thanet.

The tinker went down to Thanet to join his friend in the hunting of six bears and lions which continued to cause mischief and it was on this expedition that Henry Nonsuch was killed. The distraught Sir Thomas returned to the Isle of Ely and was met by a cheering crowd. Despite his great sadness over the loss of his trusty friend, he made them his solemn promise to rid the land of evil:

'My friends, while I have strength to stand,
Most manfully I will pursue
All dangers, till I clear this land
Of lions, bears and tigers too.

This you'll find true, or I'm to blame
Let it remain upon record:
Tom Hickathrift's most glorious fame,
Who never yet has broke his word!'

Not long after this determined statement he sought his final resting place. He flung a large stone with all his might, saying that wherever it landed would be his burial place. The missile travelled about five miles, and ended up in the Tilney All Saints' churchyard. There is now a splendid sign outside the church, donated by the Women's Institute, which has Tom standing with his cartwheel and axle-tree.

We are not told how or when our good giant died. All we know is his story, which has traces of other children's nursery characters, including Robin Hood who fired an arrow to mark his burial place, and the Cornish Jack the Giant Killer.

Some solar mythologists however believe that Tom's story

is far older and that initially he was a Celtic sun god, whose wheel and axle-tree represent the sun and its rays. The Smeeth or common was inundated by the waters of the Wash which the sun, alias Hickathrift, drove away to form good grazing land. When A. M. McCrae gave his lecture to the Fenland Historical Society in May 1968 entitled *The Origins of Hickathrift* he put forward his belief that 'Hiccathrift' or 'Hiccafrith' would seem to mean 'The trust of the Hiccas or Iceni' and would probably have been their god. The Iceni were a Celtic tribe who occupied eastern England before the Romans. 'His name would seem to be an Anglo-Saxon explanation, "He is the god the Hiccas trust in." '

Whether or not Sir Thomas Hickathrift was a Celtic sun god, a once-upon-a-time amalgam of heroes, or just a ripping yarn, his memory belongs to Cambridgeshire and Norfolk to pass to future generations.

The
Ely and Littleport
Riots

THERE is a stone inscription in St Mary's church, Ely which states:

'Here lye interred in one grave the bodies of William Beamiss, George Crow, John Dennis, Isaac Harley and Thomas South, who were all executed at Ely on the 28th day of June, 1816, having been convicted at the Special Assizes holden there of divers robberies during the riots at Ely and Littleport in the month of May in that year. May their awful fate be a warning to others.'

The riots were a protest against the harsh conditions brought with the aftermath of the Napoleonic Wars in 1815, when unemployment, hunger and poverty were rife. A series of poor harvests had caused severe food shortages and the 1815 Corn Laws guaranteed to keep the price of wheat at a high level. The Industrial Revolution was making many traditional jobs redundant and now the returning soldiers were competing for too few jobs and wages were low. In rural areas the Enclosure Acts were making the division between landowner and landworker even greater, as most commonland was taken from the people and absorbed into the new field structures. This removal of ancient rights spelled disaster to many people who were reliant upon the common land for grazing their animals, both for food and profit.

In line with landworkers from many country areas throughout England, the people of Cambridgeshire held protest rallies against these terrible conditions. Their anger was mainly directed towards the large landowners whose wealth was steadily increasing. Haystacks were fired and machinery smashed and the cries of 'Bread or blood!' echoed throughout East Anglia.

Small owner and tenant farmers could no longer meet their overheads and men were laid off work. Some were forced into road mending at 2/6d a week, others took up begging, whilst others starved along with their families. During the first year of peace the average wage for farm labourers in this county was between eight shillings and nine shillings a week. Some lived rent-free whilst others paid about a shilling a week in rent, and by May a loaf of bread cost 11¾d.

This is the scenario which led to the Ely and Littleport Riots in 1816, the severest of all the many East Anglian uprisings. This was not the work of seasoned political activists, but the desperate action of half-starved male and female landworkers who were seeking cheaper food, more work, better wages and an increase in the allowance for the unemployed. Their anger and frustration had been simmering for a long time.

On 22nd May some 60 men gathered in the Globe Inn, Littleport where they were to meet a small group of men who had recently led rioting in Denver and Southery (Norfolk) and were to help the Littleport people plan their own campaign. The meeting was specially arranged to take place on 'Club Night', when the landlord paid out one shilling to each member of the savings club. When the Norfolk men failed to turn up, emotions were so highly charged, doubtless helped by the unaccustomed quantity of beer purchased with the savings money, that the crowd decided to take immediate action by themselves.

A small group of men was deputed to call upon the unpopular local vicar and magistrate, the Rev John Vatchell, to demand that he call a special meeting that very evening with his fellow magistrates to negotiate the same concessions as had recently been granted at Downham Market and Brandon. Vatchell dismissed them without discussion and locked his door.

Tempers raged inside the Globe Inn when the vicar's cavalier attitude was reported back to the impatient landworkers and at about eight o'clock they took to the streets chanting repeatedly, 'A day's work for a stone of flour'. Someone had brought along a big hunting horn which was used when taking pleasure trips down the river Ouse and its loud hoots soon brought many more men and women onto the streets. They bumped into Mr Henry Martin, a most unpopular, wealthy, biblethumping farmer, magistrate and parish councillor. He was also an overseer of the parish relief and was forever voicing his opinion that this relief was more than enough to meet the needs of poor people. Faced with this crowd of angry people he offered the mob the following deal which appeared on posters throughout the village the next day. However this offer was too little and came too late:

'The MAGISTRATES agree, and do ORDER, that the OVERSEERS shall pay to each poor Family Two SHILLINGS per Head per Week, when FLOUR is Half-a-Crown a Stone, such Allowance to be raised in Proportion when the Price of Flour is higher, and that the Price of Labour shall be Two Shillings per Day, whether Married or Single, and that the Labourer shall be paid his full Wages by the Farmer who Hires him.

No Person to be prosecuted for any thing that has been done to the present Time; provided that every MAN immediately returns peaceably to his own Home.
Ely, May 23, 1816'

The magistrates immediately called a meeting with the principal residents and soon many tradespeople were being sworn in as special constables. A messenger was swiftly dispatched to alert the dragoons stationed in Bury St Edmunds, and the magistrate and one-time editor of the *Morning Post*, Sir Bates Dudley, together with Reverend Henry Law, rector of Denver were elected to supervise the action.

Dozens of eye witnesses later gave their account of the affray, which involved the mob first stoning the windows and looting all the stock from the Littleport shops, eating and drinking whatever was available. The next target was the homes of the wealthy, whose doors were hacked down and windows broken. If their demands for food, drink and money were not granted, they stole all that they could carry and totally vandalised the place. Sallis, the servant of Mr Henry Martin told the court at the subsequent trial how Richard Jessop had broken the back door of his master's house with a crow-bar. The family had long since fled, but had left £5 with the servant to appease the mob. Jessop had replied that he would not stop for money, he wanted Martin. The house was full of rioters who proceeded to hack the furniture to pieces with a cleaver.

Rioting went on in this vein throughout the night and at about five o'clock the next mornng they set off to neighbouring Ely, some riding in a big wagon pulled by two horses. A big punt or 'Fen Wash' gun, charged with heavy slugs was mounted to the front and back of the vehicle, which was manned by 'pot valiant Fenmen.' Their makeshift weapons included forks, cleavers, knives and bludgeons and their intention was to 'cut down every soldier they met', which certainly never happened. They also intended to get the people of Ely out onto the streets. Soon this fine city resembled Littleport on the previous evening. Landlords and the local brewery were forced to hand over their barrels of beer, which were tapped with great relish.

The wagon was stationed outside the Lamb Inn and at

about noon the dragoons rode in, led by Sir Bates Dudley. They must have looked a terrifying sight as they rode up the Gallery, their drawn swords flashing in the sunlight. The Fenmen did not stand a chance and soon the crowd had scattered in all directions, with the Littleport people heading back for home. The soldiers managed to grab some of the rioters, who were thrown into a wagon and flogged through the streets of Ely. Dudley's Ride, as it became known, spread terror in the hearts of these country folk.

Once Ely was subdued the soldiers set off for Littleport, where they met little organised resistance. Some of the now exhausted men tried to knock the soldiers off their mounts and one, Thomas Sindall, took a pot shot at a dragoon and wounded his arm. Another soldier shot back in retaliation and the slug went right through Sindall's head and was embedded in a wooden door post. Although there were several casualties, this was the only recorded death throughout the duration of the upheavals.

A total of some 100 prisoners were locked in Ely gaol and a Special Assize Court was set up in the city to try the accused, which opened on Monday, 17th June. Before the start of the proceedings a service was held in Ely Cathedral, where the three justices, in the company of 50 principal persons and the Bishop of Ely, all processed down the aisle to the triumphal anthem, *Why do the Heathen Rage?* The trial lasted five days and the scores of accounts of intimidation, looting and vandalism made sad hearing. As so many people were involved it was decided to make severe pronouncements upon the ring-leaders and to set the remaining prisoners free, to remember forever the 'terrible warning.'

On Saturday 22nd June it was announced that 24 people, including one woman, Sarah Hobbs, were to be hanged. In the end only five of the condemned were executed, the others including Mrs Hobbs having their sentences commuted to imprisonment ranging from twelve months, and transportation from between 14 years and life. A few weeks later the prison sentences were further commuted to seven years transportation, with the prisoners having already set sail before their families were told.

A large and sympathetic crowd watched the execution on Friday 28th June, 1816 of William Beamiss, George Crow, John Dennis, Isaac Harley and Thomas South, who were all hanged on a specially built gallows near Mill Pits, Ely. There were few in the crowd who did not have some family connection with the uprising.

Their awful fate was not really a warning to others for disturbances occurred throughout the county for another 18 years, although the people of Ely and Littleport remained silent. The years after the accession of Queen Victoria brought a gradual improvement in conditions, the Corn Laws were repealed in 1846 and by 1872 Agricultural Welfare Societies, the forerunners of trade unions, had come to Cambridgeshire. Now the landworkers had a formal channel of communication.

Until quite recently the Transport and General Workers Union had a rest home for their members at Littleport, which was a great tribute to those who lost their lives and suffered so desperately in the name of agricultural progress.

A
Burwell
Alphabet

NO mention is made of the author of this delightful alphabet which is dated 1862 and has been copied from the unpublished Village Notebooks compiled by Miss Edith Porter, the one-time curator of the Cambridge Folk Museum. She died some years ago after spending much of her life studying and collecting the folk history and customs of Cambridgeshire and wrote several books on these subjects.

The alphabet and its key poke gentle fun at some of the citizens of the Fen village of Burwell, which lies some twelve miles east of Cambridge and four miles north of Newmarket. The author had no malicious intentions but an apparent talent for one-line character assessment. It is printed here by kind permission of the Cambridge Folk Museum.

A   was an Anderson, lazy and slow.
B   was Tom Ball and Richard the Co.
C   were the Casburns of whom there are flocks.
D   was a Danby who lived at the Fox.
E   was Miss Eastwell whom Martin did charm her.
F   was a Fuller who once was a farmer.
G   was a Gardiner, a builder not quick.
H   was a Hunt, a layer of brick.

I   was an innkeeper, John Carter they call.
J   was Tom Johnson of Tunbridge and Hall.
K   was Joe Kent who of draughts took enough.
L   was a Lucas, a taker of snuff.
M   was a Mingay, whose bus was his life.
N   was Jack Nichols, chastising his wife.
O   was an Oliver, a grinder of flour.
P   was John Peachey, right High Chancellor.
Q   was a query if Fielder was right.
R   was a rubicund, joyous and bright.
S   was a stays, an artist self-made.
T   was a Turner by name and by trade.
U   was an umpire, who never was wrong.
V   was a vicar both hearty and strong.
W   was Sweet William whose surname was Dunn.
X   the expense attending his fund.
Y   were the youths of Burwell, far famed.
Z   we leave for want of a name.

This is the key to the Alphabet:

A   Issac Anderson. One of the cricket team, good but a slack fielder.
B   Mr T. T. Ball. Chemical manure manufacturer who had recently taken his brother Richard into partnership and was known by his friends as 'The Co.'
C   Casburns. Very numerous in the village.
D   William Danby. Kept the Fox Inn, one of the best conducted in the village and where meetings, sales and public dinners were held.
E   Miss Eastwell. Greatly admired by William Martin the carpenter.
F   Will Fuller. Who sold his land and farm to Thomas Lucas.
G   Mr Gardiner. A good builder and contractor but thought to be slow.

H   John Hunt. Master craftsman in brick-laying.

I   John Carter. A brewer, maltster and proprietor of the White Horse. Considered to be a good judge of horseflesh and well-known by dealers who stayed at his house for Reach Fair.

J   Thomas Johnson. Lived at the Hall and was a frequent visitor at the Tunbridge Inn and was thought to be a representative of both houses.

K   Joe Kent. Wealthy farmer of Swaffham Prior who suffered from nerves. He liked to see his doctor each morning and took four draughts of medicine daily.

L   Thomas Lucas. Snuff taker. He owned a box with a polished Scottish pebble set in silver.

M   Henry Mingay. He was a thrifty yeoman farmer who had a carrier's cart and drove a bus named 'Perseverance'. A cheery fellow.

N   Jack Nicholas. The pork butcher who loved strong ale and beat his wife when drunk.

O   Oliver Carter. Stout old miller, wore a white hat and brought grist to his mill in a yellow cart with red shafts and wheels.

P   John Peachey. A big old man who once appeared, with others, at a London law court on a charge of not paying his lawful dues on his farmland. The knowledge of lawyers and the law that he acquired there was vast. When he was excited his gesticulations were so violent that he was given the name 'Lord Chancellor.'

Q   Mr Fielder. Graduate of Jesus College, Cambridge, used to spend months together at the Five Miles From Anywhere Inn at Upware and from the inn's patrons formed a republic and made himself president. His satirical remarks on some of the Fen magnates made them question if he were in his right mind.

R   Rubicund Mr Bob Peachey. 'Bustling old stock,' a jobber with a smile and cheery word.

S   Will Peachey. The village fop, reputed to have worn stays.

He was infatuated with a lady and used to paint her portrait and put it in her summerhouse.

T Will Turner. Clever manipulator of words. He often said, 'I never go to church when there is a gathering. I don't hold with the University taking £6,000 a year out of the parish without paying all dues and demands.'

U Bill Dunn. His knowledge of cricket was very limited. He was an umpire who would never admit that he gave a wrong ruling.

V The Reverend Crockholt. A man of great energy and endurance. He restored the church, built schools and did much for young people.

W Mr Will Dunn. His brown rubicund and gnarled face suggested the Sweet William flower as it faded.

X Mr Dunn. The treasurer of the cricket club, whose own expenses in collecting the subscriptions had to be considered.

Y Youths of Burwell. More harmless fun of Burwell celebrities.

Hobson's Choice

THE adage 'Hobson's Choice', meaning no choice whatsoever, was built around an honest, hardworking and shrewd Cambridge man called Thomas Hobson, who had a carrier's business and livery stable, originally housed on a site which fronted onto Trumpington Street and now forms part of Catherine's College. He was a humane person who insisted that all his hiring horses should be taken in strict rotation and no matter how influential the customer, it always had to be the horse which 'stood next the stable door'. This was Hobson's choice and by using such a system he considered, 'Everyone was alike well served according to his chance and every horse ridden with the same justice.'

Thomas Hobson was born in 1544 at Buntingford, Hertfordshire to Thomas and Elinor Hobson and was the eldest of their eight humbly educated children. Hobson senior operated a small carrier's business in Hertfordshire, which he brought with him when the family moved to Cambridge in 1561. Young Thomas worked with his father, from whom he inherited the business upon his death in 1568. This comprised, 'The team ware that he now goeth with, that is to say, the cart and eight horses, and all the harness and other things thereunto belonging with the nag. . .'

Hobson was to continue in this trade for a further 63 years, carrying between Cambridge and the Bull Inn, Bishopsgate, London. In the early days transportation by a wagon and team was still an innovative service, as most trading was still done by pack-horse. This new and efficient method was soon

in great demand and his wagons were shortly delivering goods and passengers to most parts of East Anglia, in addition to the London route. He was obviously a pioneer in the world of transport and his wealth continued to grow, helped by his frugal life-style.

Although Hobson was very careful with his money, never spending unwisely that which could be saved, he was a very public spirited man whose generosity to the town has helped preserve his name. In 1574, with the support of several other like-minded people, he was instrumental in bringing fresh water to Cambridge from the Nine Wells on Shelford Moor.

The water came via a three mile long artificial waterway known as 'Hobson's River' and in 1614 he financed a water conduit which was built in the Market Place. This was an hexagonal shaped stone building, decorated with simple carvings, with a giant golden coloured pineapple on top and enclosed with an iron palisade. The water ran continuously through four water spouts which supplied the neighbourhood with a never failing stream of water. This remained in situ until 1856 when it was moved to Brookside, at the junction of Trumpington Street and Lensfield Road, where it still stands.

Thomas Hobson bequeathed seven leys of pasture in this area to trustees to provide the perpetual maintenance of the conduit. This land was known as the Swinescroft and the leys were lammas lands, which means the owners had exclusive rights from the spring until Lammas Day, 1st August. It was then opened up for the remaining eight months to be grazed by the animals of those who possessed lammas rights. These leys were held until 1801, when a private Act of Parliament released them for sale and they were purchased for the original site and grounds of Downing College.

His philanthropy extended to his conveyance of a piece of land, in July 1628, to the town and university, situated in the Market Place. This was for the erection of what was officially known as The Spinning House, and unofficially as 'Hobson's Workhouse'. This was where the poor and out of work could find employment as spinners. Later a semi-penal wing, known as a Bridewell was added where 'stubborn rogues and beggars', who refused to work could be committed.

An article appeared in the *Gentleman's Magazine* in 1802 which gave a detailed account of the Spinning House:

'Cambridge Town Bridewell is a square building surrounded by a boundary wall of 15 feet high and about 5 feet from the prison; was originally bought and endowed for the encouragement of wool-combers and spinners of this town. . . . . . To answer the intention, the keeper is a wool-comber. He employs not only several hands upon the foundation of the charity, but many others; among them his prisoners. . . . . . Each cell has a mattress, two blankets, and a rug. For men there are three cells at the entrance, each 9 feet by 7½ feet, and near 8 feet high, with straw on the floor. A tub serves the purpose of a necessary in these cells. They are ventilated by an iron grating over each door which has an aperture about 6 inches square. For women there are ten cells, the same size as the men's and four court-yards with a privy in each. There is only one pump in the prison. Many of the cells are out of repair, and the whole prison very dirty.'

In its latter years the building was used as a place of confinement 'Of such lewd women as the Proctors apprehend in houses of ill fame; though sometimes the Corporation send small offenders thither, and the crier of the town is often there to discipline the ladies of pleasure with his whip.' In 1865 the Bridewell was merged into the prison system and the building was demolished in 1901.

Like Thomas senior, Hobson was also the father of eight children born to him by his first wife, Ann, who died in 1615. As his wealth increased he invested a lot of his money in property and over the years bought the two principal manors in Cottenham and the priory and manor of Anglesey. He also leased the manors of Waterbeach and Denny.

By the middle of 1630 the authorities had stopped all travelling to London, which was suffering from the ravages of the plague, and this old man of almost 86 years was no longer able to make his regular journey from Cambridge to the Bull Inn, Bishopsgate. One wonders how such an ancient person could have made these slow and lengthy trips, but he did, and when deprived his health went into a decline. On 1st January, 1631 he died of ennui.

The poet Milton who had gone up to Christ's College in 1624, wrote two rather flippant epitaphs on this well respected old man. One was entitled *On the University Carrier who sickened in the time of the Vacancy, being forbid to go to London by reason of the Plague*, and made obvious reference to the dangers of his trade:

'Death was half glad when he had got him down
For he had any time this ten year full
Dodged with him betwixt Cambridge and the Bull.'

A more reverent tribute was made by one of the carrier's contemporaries, who remains anonymous:

'Mr Hobson, the carrier of Cambridge, by the help of common prudence and constant attention to a few frugal maxims, raised a much greater fortune than a thousand men of genius and learning, educated in that university, ever acquired, or were even capable of acquiring.'

The great man was laid to rest in the chancel of St Benedict's by Market Hill on 12th January 1631, but the spot bears no memorial. However his name lives on in Hobson Street and through the water conduit, which indeed was Hobson's own choice.

Stourbridge Fair

UNTIL the end of the Middle Ages most trade in this country and especially foreign trade, was undertaken at fairs. Foreigners were restricted from buying and selling in chartered towns so fairs were ideal venues where they used the money earned from their sales to buy goods for export.

These trading fairs helped towns to develop and obviously played an important role in the nation's economy, with events such as Stourbridge Fair attracting merchants and buyers from all over England and the world. The river Granta (now the Cam) flows along one side of the site and greatly helped with the transportation of materials and visitors.

Its site was at Stourbridge Common, Barnwell, near Cambridge and the fair is believed to have started on a small scale sometime during the reign of King Athelstan (AD 925–940) when Irish cloth merchants met for two days to buy and sell their merchandise. Over the centuries the fair grew both in size and duration, expanding with the growth of the University and in its heyday lasting three weeks.

King John granted a market charter in 1211, its profits to be given to the lepers of the hospital of St Mary Magdalene at Stourbridge. In 1539 the rights and profits were commuted to the Corporation of Cambridge by King Henry VIII, and the charter was confirmed by Queen Elizabeth I in about 1588.

From 1533 to 1855 the opening or proclamation of the market was made by the Corporation and the University, the latter calling it on odd numbered years. Its duration was from the Feast of St Bartholomew, 24th August to the Feast of St

Michael the Archangel, or Michaelmas Day, 29th September. If the corn was not cleared from the land by 24th August the fair-organisers had the right to trample over it. Conversely if the fair was not cleared by Michaelmas Day the farmers who rented the common land had the right to plough down the booths and tents.

The fairground was set out to resemble a miniature city, with streets being allotted to each individual trade, so the hatters were in one street, the drapers in another, etc. A plan of 1725 shows areas for the coal fair, one for the ironsmiths, and tallow makers at Tallow Hill. There is Brazier's Row, Bookseller's Row, White Leather Fair, the Horse Fair, Cheese and Garlic Rows, the Pot Fair, Wool Fair and others, including the Duddery or Cloth Fair. All the trades were housed in booths or tents, some being divided into apartments.

There was a wide choice of eating and drinking houses and amusement booths such as cheap toys, puppet shows and 'drolls and rope-dancing'. Order was maintained by the fair's special court known as the 'Court of Piepowder', administered by the Mayor and his eight red-coated sergeants known as 'Redcoats'. Their job was to settle any disputes which arose between the traders and buyers. If tempers flared all somebody had to do was to yell 'Redcoat! Redcoat!' and help was soon to hand.

The 'Lord of the Taps' was appointed to make sure that the ale sold in the booths was in good condition and he too wore a red coat, but decorated with barrel taps. In 1700 he was described as 'Arm'd all over with spiggots and fossets like a porcupine with his quills, or looking rather like a fowl wrapped in a pound of sausages.' A spigot was a small wooden peg or pin used to bung up the vent hole of a barrel or cask and a 'fosset' was really a faucet or tap used for drawing off the liquor from a barrel.

The vast numbers of booth holders and visitors must have posed as many problems for the people of Barnwell as the visitors to pop festivals do today when converging on small rural communities. Feeding and hygiene must have been real problems, even if the latter was ever considered. The 1725 site plan shows no marked privies or latrines, which if they were provided must have competed with the stench of dung from the hordes of pack-horses used for transporting goods. The fair which Daniel Defoe visited had more than 1,000 pack-horses for the cloth traders alone. Their manure was known as 'Farmers Fees' and was compensation for the damage and inconvenience caused by the fair.

The merchants and stallholders slept in their booths, which were made from hair cloth which was hardly waterproof. Their beds were made from two or three planks nailed together, with a plank edging to stop the occupant rolling out. Crude legs were nailed to the corners to raise the beds off the ground.

Daniel Defoe wrote an account of the fair in his *Tour Through the Eastern Counties* printed in 1724. He was very impressed by what he experienced, especially the Duddery or Cloth Fair. This square was flanked on all sides with large booths, occupied by wholesale cloth merchants and tailors.

'Here the Booths, or Tents are of a vast Extent, having different Appartments, and the Quantities of Goods they bring are so Great, that the Insides of them look like another "Blackwell Hall", being as vast Ware-houses pil'd up with Goods to the Top. In this Duddery, as I have been inform'd, have been sold £100,000 worth of Woollen Manufactures in less than a Week's time; besides the prodigious Trade carry'd on here, by Wholesale-men from London, and all Parts of England, who transact their Business wholly in their Pocket-Books, and meeting their Chapmen from all Parts, make up their accounts, receive Money chiefly in Bills, and take Orders. These they say exceed by far the Sale of Goods actually brought to the Fair, and deliver'd in Kind; it being frequent for the London Wholesale-men to carry back Orders from their Dealers for

£10,000 worth of Goods a Man, and some much more. This especially respects those People who deal in heavy Goods as Wholesale Grocers, Salters, Brasiers, Iron Merchants and especially in Mercery Goods of all sorts, the dealers in which generally managed their business in this manner.'

The trade in wool, hops and leather was also prodigious, the value of wool sold at one fair was worth between £50,000 and £60,000 and of hops only a little less.

The Horse Fair was held on 14th September and always attracted a huge crowd, who ate their way through quantities of Colchester oysters and white herring which were just coming into season. They were a special delicacy to land-locked people who rarely had a chance to sample such morsels.

Like most good things, Stourbridge Fair had to come to an end. The growth of large towns and cities and more efficient standards of trading eventually made such fairs unnecessary. By the end of the 18th century there was less emphasis on trade and more on amusement. Its decline continued so that in 1930 when the Mayor made his usual proclamation, he had an audience of six and a few swinging boats powered by a traction engine. The Mayor of 1933 fared worse, when he could only command the attention of two nursing mothers and a seller of ice-creams! They were the last witnesses of the Stourbridge Fair opening ceremony.

Hags
and
Heathens

A few centuries ago various people who travelled to the Northern Fens were quite amazed at what they saw. They made some harsh and sweeping comments in the privacy of their diaries about both the people and their environment. One has to bear in mind that the Fens of two or three centuries ago were waterlogged and communities were isolated. The Fen people were an independent race and would have treated these 'foreigners' with great caution.

Samuel Pepys, Secretary to the Admiralty, often visited the county as his parents owned a large manor in Cottenham and he had been educated at Huntingdon grammar school. On one occasion he came to Parson Drove with an uncle and cousin to discuss family business with his Uncle and Aunt Perkins, who lived in poverty in this Fen village. His Aunt Beatrice had recently inherited a lot of wealth from their relation John Day of Wisbech, which was a matter of some concern to Samuel. Aunt Perkins was his mother's sister and it offended his somewhat snobbish nature to see her living under thatch, which according to him was a most common thing to do in the 17th century!

The visitors arrived in Parson Drove on 17th September 1663 where they put up in the Swan Inn. Pepys' diary entry is as follows:

'I begun a journey with them [uncle and cousin] and with much ado, through the fenns, along dikes, where sometimes we were ready to have our horses sink to the belly, we got by night with a great deal of stir, and hard riding to Parson's Drove, a heathen place, where I found my uncle and aunt Perkins and their daughters, poor wretches — in a sad poor thatched cottage like a poor barn or stable, peeling of hemp, and in a poor condition of habitt took them to our miserable inne, and after a long stay and hearing of Frank, their son, the miller, play upon his treble, as he calls it, with which he earns part of his living, and singing of a country song, we set down to supper, the whole crew and Frank's wife and child, a sad company, of which I was ashamed, supped with us. By and by news is brought to us that one of our horses is stole out of the stable, which proves my uncle's, at which I am inwardly glad; I mean that it was not mine. And so about twleve at night or more, to bed, in a sad cold stony chamber; and a little while after I was asleep, they waked me to tell me that the horse was found, which was good news, and so to sleep but was bit sadly, and nobody else of our company, which I wonder at, by the gnatts. Up and got our people together, and after eating a dish of cold creame, which was my supper last night too, we took leave of our beggardly company, though they seem good people too; and over more sad fenns, all the way observing the sad life which the people of the place; which if they be born there they do call the Breedlings of the place; do live, sometimes rowing from one spot to another, and then wadeing.'

The natives had names other than 'Breedlings'. Those who dwelled in the wet areas were known as 'Fen Slodgers': people who walked about on stilts and vaulted streams and dykes with their long poles. Some slodgers were reputed to have webbed feet, which could have been some congenital defect. The 'Yellow Bellies' were the inhabitants of the Lincolnshire border and on into that neighbouring county. They earned this name from the habit of the women who hitched their skirts high to warm themselves over their turf fires. The smoke stained their skins yellow.

Another tourist with a harsh pen was Celia Fiennes, an intrepid lady traveller who toured England on horseback in 1696. She had been nearly thrown from her mount as she rode along the causeway to Ely and later wrote that the town was 'The dirtiest place I ever saw, not a bit of pitching in the streets except around the [Bishop's] Palace and the churches. The Bishop does not care to stay long in this place not being for his health.' In her opinion the men were, 'A slothful people and for little but the taking care of their grounds and cattle.'

Some of the most spectacular visitors to the region must have been Lord Orford, Lord of the Bedchamber to King George III, and his fellow sailors who made their 'Voyage round the Fens' commencing 17th July, 1774. They were accommodated in a fleet of nine fen lightercraft, towed by a large horse called Hippopotamus (which is Greek for 'river horse'). Accompanying him was his mistress Martha Turk and various influential friends, some of whom joined him in keeping a record of the voyage. His route took in Outwell, March, Whittlesey Mere, Peterborough, Benwick and then back up the river Ouse to Lakenheath in Suffolk.

To be fair, these part-time mariners did find plenty to praise, but they also made some pompous and scathing re-marks concerning the appearance of the Fen people and their environment which today sound quite amusing. Their first trip took them through Nordelph (Norfolk), Outwell, Upwell and March which they considered to be 'four fair and handsome Towns . . . The Churches are large and well built, the houses clean, but the inhabitants meanly clad and dirty, and, being on account of the day unemployed assembled in crowds on both sides of the River to view and admire so uncommon a sight.'

Another entry concerning Outwell states, 'It is equally remarkable for the ugliness of the inhabitants as for the handsomeness of the church — a disagreeable sallow complexion, broad flat nose, and wide mouth predominating among them.' In Lord Orford's opinion there were 'Many very old women in Upwell, Outwell and March; the sex in general extremely ugly.'

The Ramsey (Old Huntingdonshire) people were paid a back-handed compliment for although they were penned as Bohemian rabbits they were voted the best of the Fen bunch! 'The people are remarked as having long teeth and strait lank hair, which did not prevent our giving them the preference to the inhabitants of all other Fen towns we passed, which compliment was extended to the place itself.'

However, later in the journey Ramsey town lost out to March, 'Which is the best town we have seen in the voyage. There are many good houses, and the town in general was well built. There are gardens before most houses, which run down to the waterside, and greatly added to our pleasure by the variety of colours their borders afforded.' The March people lost hands down on looks compared with Ramsey, for on another day, 'We passed through March at twelve, and examining the people separately, found we had no reason to alter our former opinion relative to that disagreeable arrangement of features called ugliness, entailed upon them.'

It was comments such as these that fuelled inter-village and town rivalry for countless years! Communities filled with broad nosed, big mouthed ugly women have long since disappeared and Parson Drove is no longer a 'heathen place' but an attractive village and winner of Best Kept Village competitions.

The Country Calendar

BEFORE modern technology and chemistry irrevocably changed the rural scene most country dwellers throughout the county worked in agriculture. Although their old calendar customs had been dwindling since the turn of the 20th century they were still upheld in many villages until about the 1950s, when new work patterns and access to entertainment lessened the importance of these old delights. However, many towns and villages are now reviving the Plough Monday celebrations as folk festivals, with rarely a landworker to be seen.

Plough Monday, the first Monday after Twelfth Night, when the farm labourers returned to work was the first highspot in the new year. In pre-tractor days it was customary for ploughmen to be on the land from harvest right through to the spring sowing, weather permitting of course. Some men took the day off on Plough Monday, others having their fun after work. Either way the old school log books show a high rate of absenteeism when the children went out to watch their elders making fools of themselves. This was the day when men blackened up their faces, and some wore women's clothes, to provide a good camouflage for when they went out demanding their largesse. Many villages throughout the county called their men dressed in this fashion 'Plough Witches' and indulged their high spirits, which often got out of hand.

There was an unwritten gentlemen's agreement that Plough Witches never strayed over parish boundaries, but this was not always so, as recorded in 1850 when the Ramsey, Old Huntingdonshire, men went into Benwick, Cambridgeshire and vice versa and 'severe encounters took place.'

The men pulled an old plough behind them or towed a mock wooden one and were often accompanied by a team of Morris dancers and a 'Molly' who was a man dressed as a woman. They must have looked a fantastic sight as they made their noisy way around the village, calling on houses and rattling their collecting tins, which would be emptied in the pub later that day. Any miserly person who refused largesse was in danger of having one of the 'witches' remove 'her' knickers and wrap them around his mean neck! More than likely the men would plough up part of his front garden with their plough or dig a swathe with a spade. Throughout the celebrations the Plough Monday song would be sung by the ploughmen and there were many versions used throughout the county. The following two verses from the Yelling, Old Huntingdonshire area was a popular rendition used with some modifications in many villages:

'Early one morn at the break of the day
When the cocks were all crowing the farmer did say
Come rise my good fellows, come rise with good will
For your horses want something their bellies to fill.

'When four o'clock comes boys when us we must rise
And into the stable so merrily fly
With rubbing and scrubbing our horses I'll vow
That we're all jolly fellows that follow the plough.'

Ploughmen and Morris dancers from some villages close to Cambridge, such as Girton, Maddingley and Histon, left home early on Plough Monday morning calling on their own communities and then dancing into Cambridge where they met up in the Market Place in the late afternoon. By the beginning of this century this revelry had turned into nothing less than a drunken brawl and was stopped by the authorities.

Plough Monday fun had its roots in an ancient fertility ritual, the dancing, change of sex and mock or real ploughing being imitative magic to ensure the seed for the next harvest would be well bedded in good soil and produce a plentiful crop. In many parishes it was traditional for ploughs to be taken to church for their annual blessing on the Sunday before Plough Monday. This was part of the general respect afforded to the land when it was regarded as a living partner of the farmer, the true Mother Earth, which was nurtured with care. Bassingbourne, Duxford and Dry Drayton kept their parish plough, which could be hired by any parishioner, in their church for safe keeping.

Whittlesey and Ramsey deferred their plough revels until the next day which was 'Straw Bear Tuesday'. The custom was stopped in Ramsey at the end of the 19th century and in Whittlesey a few years later. In the case of the latter town the reason given was that it had got out of hand and there was too much drinking and scandalous behaviour. Happily the custom was revived in 1979 and takes place on the Saturday after Plough Monday. The 'bear' and his entourage parade the streets, but in a more orderly fashion and their largesse goes to charity.

The *Peterborough Advertiser* dated 16th January 1866 gave a good account of the Ramsey 'bear' and his merry-making and the Whittlesey 'bear' is made in a similar fashion today:

'Great lengths of tightly twisted straw bands were prepared and the boy chosen was completely wound up in them, arms and legs separately. Two sticks fastened to his shoulders met in a point above his head and the straw was wound up on them to form a cone above the 'bear's' head. The face was quite covered and he could hardly see. A tail was provided and a strong chain fastened round his armpits. On approaching a house the 'bear' would go down on his hands and knees and growl and groan as the door was opened, while those accompanying him would pretend to check him by pulling at the chain and by blows with a light stick. It was great fun frightening the servant girls, and on one occasion a girl strange to the district fainted. . .'

The next major agricultural event following haymaking in June was harvesting, which usually started on Lammas Day, 1st August weather permitting. Before mechanisation this was a labour intensive season and the farmers hired extra hands from outside the area. These men, who were often accompanied by their families, came to the same farm for years on end and were usually accommodated in bothies and slept on straw palliasses. Farmers quite welcomed heavy drinkers just so long as it did not hinder the man's work, because it meant that he spent his wages very quickly and would need to stay on and work to get more money.

Still into this century it was usual for the farmers to get together with their men on the day before harvest started to negotiate a fair wage for the season's work. Often one man was elected to speak for the men, who became 'Lord of the Harvest' for that year and acted as their supervisor and negotiator.

Thomas Tusser (1524–1580) refers to such a person in his verse:

'Grant harvest lord, more by a penny or two,
to call on his fellows the better to do;
Give gloves to thy reapers, a largess to cry,
and daily to loiterers have a good eye.'

Work started each day soon after sunrise and lasted until dusk. To ensure the workers turned up on time some South Cambridgeshire villages had a man or boy go round the village blowing a tin horn at dawn. William King of Melbourn, who died in 1935 at the age of 84 years, had blown the harvest horn from the age of seven.

In Little Shelford the Lord 'shoed' each new worker in the harvest field. He aped the blacksmith by banging a stone on the sole of the newcomer's shoe, demanding the payment of one shilling which went into the beer fund.

In the Northern Fens many women made special harvest 'Fleed Cakes'. These were ordinary large fruit cakes but instead of using butter or margarine they substituted fleed, which surrounds pigs' kidneys. This hard white fat made a very good cake but was only used during this season. Slices of cake would be placed alongside refreshing bottles of cold tea and taken out to the men in the harvest field in time for their tea break or 'foursies'. Food was always carried in 'flaggin' baskets', made from rush with a hinged lid and carrying handle.

Bringing in the last load, known as the 'Harvest Horkey', was always a time for great rejoicing. Until the beginning of this century the cart was decorated with boughs of greenery and flowers. In the south a pretty girl or 'Harvest Queen' presided over the last load, but up in the north it was usually the youngest working boy who sang a song something along the lines of:

'Harvest Home! Harvest Home!
Two plum puddings are better than one,
We've plowed, we've sowed,
We've reaped, we've mowed,
We've got our harvest home.'

The last sheaf of corn to be cut was nearly always treated with respect as it was regarded by most communities as the embodiment of the Corn Spirit, the essence of all fruitful harvests. In the Peterborough villages it was the custom into this century to decorate this sheaf with ribbons and flowers and then fasten it to the wall of a barn until it was replaced the next year. Other farmers preferred to have its grains put inside a corn dolly cornucopia which was then hung in the farmhouse kitchen to ensure the fertility of both his family and his land.

By the end of the last century the 'Horkey Supper' was generally giving way to a harvest bonus payment, but some farms carried on with the tradition until a later date. The supper was provided by the farmer and given to all his workers, permanent and temporary, and to their wives. Long trestle tables were set up in a large barn which was decorated with sheaves of corn, fruit and flowers, rather lke a church at Harvest Festival. The traditional fare was roast beef, plum pudding and beer, all in great quantities. In the old days beef would have been an unaccustomed luxury as low pay could only stretch to a diet of pig meat.

After the supper all the trestles were cleared away for singing and dancing and lots more beer was brought in for wetting dry and dusty throats. It was customary for the oldest labourer to propose the health of the Master and Mistress, who were always present on these occasions. He would sing the Harvest Home song which went something like this:

'Here's health unto our Master the founder of the feast,
God bless his endeavours and give him increase,
And send him good crops that we may meet another year,
Here's our Master's good health boys come drink off your
    beer!

By 1875 the Horkeys in Grantchester, near Cambridge, had been replaced with bonus handouts, but until then the chorus of their traditional song was:

'So drink, boys, drink, and mind you do not spill,
For if you do you shall drink two,
For it's our Master's will.'

The song was sung as many times as there were people present and a cup of ale was handed to each man in turn who had to down it during the chorus.

Many villages are now almost deserted during the daytime and farmers have only one or two men on their permanent payroll. Other workers belong to the gang system and are bussed in to the villages in mini vans. Apart from the local gala and the odd charity or fund raising event there are no real seasons for country people to do things together. Whether or not the 'good old days' really lived up to their name is a moot point, but there were frequent times for relatively innocent fun which lifted jaded spirits in a pleasant fashion and cost little money.

The Early Years
of
Oliver Cromwell

THE register book of the now demolished church of St John the Baptist, Huntingdon bears the inscription in simple Latin, 'In the year of Our Lord 1599, Oliverus, the son of Robert Cromwell, gent, and of Elizabeth his wife, born on the 25th day of April and baptised on the 29th of the same month.' So started the life of the man who was to have such a profound effect upon the lives of so many.

The child was named after his father's eldest brother, Sir Oliver Cromwell, who lived in the splendid family house at Hinchingbrooke, on the outskirts of Huntingdon. This one-time wealthy nunnery had been given to the Cromwells by Henry VIII after the Dissolution of the Monasteries, along with other valuable property in the area.

Oliver was the fifth of ten children: three sons, two of whom died at an early age, and seven girls. The Cromwells lived a fairly quiet life in their home at 'The Friaries', which was built on the site of a 13th century Augustinian friary in the High Street of Huntingdon. Like his uncle, Oliver's father Robert was an elected member of Parliament. He was also said to manage the 'Ale Brew-House' which formed part of his wife Elizabeth's marriage dowry. This occupation was used to good effect by Oliver Cromwell's later opponents who nicknamed him 'The Brewer'. Many verses of doggerel were written lampooning the ultimate Puritan, such as

'A brewer may be as bold as Hector
And when he has drunk his cup of nectar
And as a brewer may be a Lord Protector
As nobody can deny!'

Brewing was most certainly in his stern blood, for his paternal great-great grandfather, Morgan Williams, was a brewer from Putney. He had married Katherine, the eldest daughter of Thomas Cromwell and at some unknown date the family adopted her maiden name, at the suggestion of Henry VIII.

But what of Oliver's early life? The family must have always been rather overshadowed by their rich relations living at Hinchingbrooke but his father was a kind and gentle man who enjoyed his family. There are various somewhat apoc ryphal tales concerning Oliver's childhood. There is the story that when he was a baby and staying at Hinchingbrooke, the family's pet monkey stole the sleeping child from his cradle and pranced over the roof with little Oliver clutched in its arms. Another tale has Oliver hitting the two year old Prince Charles Stuart on the nose when his father brought him to stay at Hinchingbrooke in 1603. This may well have been made up to illustrate Oliver's future bad temper and hatred of the Monarchy.

Very little has been recorded of his formative years. He was educated at the free Huntingdon grammar school, now the Cromwell Museum attached to the Hospital of St John sited in the High Street. Another of its famous pupils was Samuel Pepys of diary fame. There was just one classroom for all the pupils and its master in charge was Dr Thomas Beard, a Cambridge graduate and clergyman with strong Puritanical views, whose philosophy must have had a great influence on young Cromwell's developing mind. Dr Beard had translated from French a work entitled *The Theatre of God's Judgements*, a huge collection of punishments inflicted by the Almighty on the transgressors from His faith. At a young age his pupil could recite large tracts of the New Testament and knew most of the psalms off by heart.

However Cromwell was not a particularly studious boy, preferring sports and games to being shut up in a school room. In 1616 he entered Sidney Sussex, Cambridge.

This strongly Protestant college with a Puritan bias had been endowed by 1596 by the executors of Lady Francis Sidney, Countess of Sussex and built on the site of the former Greyfriars monastery. The college rules stated that all students should be trained to serve the English Church and it was obligatory for the Masters and Fellows to denounce the Pope. There was to be no gambling, drinking, bull or bear-baiting and the students were not permitted to wear 'long or curled locks, great ruffles or velvet pantables.'

It was later stated by his opponents that he had never been a serious university student and he had neglected his studies in favour of 'drinking, whoring and playing football.' Cromwell did not totally deny these accusations about his youthful exploits by replying firmly, 'I lived in and loved darkness and hated the light. I was a chief, the chief of sinners.'

He only spent one year up at Cambridge for upon the death of his father in 1617 he returned home to look after the affairs of his mother and seven sisters and settled down to live in this totally female environment. His mother doted on her loving only son. In 1619 he studied law at Lincoln's Inn and met his future wife Elizabeth, daughter of Sir James Bourchier. She was two years his senior and they were married at St Giles' Cripplegate on 22nd August, 1620.

The newlyweds returned to Huntingdon and in time she bore four sons and four daughters. Cromwell's income from farming appears to have been £300 a year, which was barely sufficient to maintain his county position and a growing family. His lands were mainly down to wheat and falling

66

prices struck him hard. In 1631 he moved to St Ives where he became a grazier, feeding cattle for market. In 1628 he was elected as one of the two Huntingdon representatives to Parliament where he soon became known as a violent Puritan, attacking the 'tyranny' of the High Church bishops.

It appears that during the span between his marriage and election to Parliament, he underwent the spiritual torment of 'conversion' from which he emerged convinced that he was one of God's chosen people. He was also a melancholy person, given to long bouts of depression which doubtless contributed to his hypochondria. According to his physician Dr Symcotts, he often sent for his services in the middle of the night, convinced that his death was imminent.

Cromwell's financial worries ended in 1638 when he received his expected inheritance from his maternal uncle, Thomas Steward of Ely. Cromwell moved his family to Ely and became one of its leading citizens.

But the Civil War was brewing and Cromwell was to become a key figure in the conflict between King and Parliament. His quiet country life ended for ever when he emerged as the most powerful man in England, at the head of the New Model Army which he had created. After the execution of Charles I in 1649, it was ony a matter of time before Cromwell's military dictatorship was given a constitutional basis. From 1653 to 1658 he ruled England as Protector. He died of pneumonia on 3rd September 1658 and was succeeded by his son Richard. His republic was to last for only two more years but the effects of Oliver Cromwell's rule altered the course of English history.

Death
at the
Crossroads

WHERE the A45 Cambridge to St Neots road crosses over the A14 Royston road, you will see the replica of a gibbet post standing at the Caxton crossroads. This is the site of the original gallows which stood on part of the old common and King's Field. The structure was probably owned by the Crown for although the Abbot of Ramsey had the power to hang people, his authority fell just short of this point. This is an open, unsheltered spot and it is easy to imagine the old gibbet cage creaking in the high winds as it rocked its gruesome contents without mercy, a dreadful warning to all would-be miscreants.

The prisoner was placed alive in the cage, his head clasped firmly in an iron device secured to the top of the structure, denying any sitting or crouching to relieve aching limbs. Death would be slow, first a searing thirst and then starvation or exposure depending upon the season. Then the birds and rats would eat their fill and still the cage would sway, until its securing bolt was cut to make way for its new occupant. It was a crime for anyone to offer sustenance to the culprit and a baker from Caxton was accused of feeding such a starving man and was hanged for the deed.

Gibbets and gallows were often sited at crossroads, not

necessarily so they could be seen by the greatest number of travellers, but as a carry over from the time when those who were denied a Christian burial were buried at crossroads. The church ruled in AD740 that all who were killed by their own hands were ineligible for burial in hallowed ground. The insane were protected from this ruling, but if insanity could not be proven the body was buried usually at night and often with a stake through its heart. In 1814 an unknown man found dying from self-administered poison, in Godmanchester Field, was buried at the crossroads leading to Offord.

There is little recorded to tell us who met their end swinging from the arm of the Caxton gallows, but in 1673 Christopher Ewings was convicted of robbery and hung in the gibbet. The youngest son of Widow Gatwood, landlady of the Red Lion at Royston, he not only helped his mother to run the inn, but also helped himself to other people's money and jewellery. He was finally caught when trying to rob the mail-boy who was travelling along Ermine Street, now the A1, and was left to feed the birds in 1754.

Up in the north of the county the gibbet stood about one mile west of the Guyhirn railway bridge, on the north bank of Morton's Leam. Four men were hanged there in the late 18th century for the murder of shepherd William Marriot, his wife and young lodger.

The four accused, James Culley, Michael Quin, Thomas Quin and Thomas Markin, were all itinerant Irish farm labourers who had come to the area for harvest work. They were indicted at Wisbech on Thursday 22nd October, 1795. They were alleged to have entered the Marriots' home in Wisbech High Fen where they brutally assaulted and killed all the occupants and then made off with some money, jewels, a few silver spoons and a coat. Most of the booty was found on them when they were apprehended in Staffordshire. Although they pleaded not guilty it did not take the jury long to make its own decision and the Chief Justice passed sentence of death upon them in the following manner:-

'James Culley, Michael Quin, Thomas Quin and Thomas Markin — you have been tried by a Jury of your Country, and found Guilty of the horrid crime of MURDER — a crime at which human nature revolts, and which is punished with Death in most countries in the world. All that now remains of my melancholy duty, is to pass the dreadful sentence of the law upon you, which is — That you [all] be taken from hence to the place from whence you came, and from thence on Saturday next to the place of execution; and that you be there hanged by the neck till you are dead, and that your bodies be delivered to the surgeons to be dissected and anatomized, pursuant to the statute in that case made and provided. And may the Lord God Almighty have Mercy on your Souls.'

The four unfortunate men were executed on the appointed day at about eight o'clock in the morning, watched by a large crowd. After hanging the usual time their bodies were cut down — two of them were given to surgeons for dissection and the other two hung in chains from the gibbet.

All evidence of the gallows has been removed but the terrain remains wild and lonely, broken only by pathways made by sheep.

Witchcraft!

THE origins of witchcraft stem from pagan fertility religions which were resistant to the early Christians'
attempts to destroy these old beliefs. The old and the new
religions co-existed for many centuries, the god of the old cult
becoming the Devil of the Christians', the worshipper becoming the witch and afforded powers of magic. The cult gra-
dually evolved into a secret society and as such not only
attracted the true believer, but also the disaffected and
immoral.

In 1644 Matthew Hopkins, the Witchfinder General, and
his fellow 'Witch Prickers' were appointed by Parliament to
scour East Anglia in search of supposed witches, which resulted in the deaths of many innocent people, most of whom
were women. Suspects were pricked all over, for it was held
that the Devil made one spot on his followers' bodies which
was immune to pain. As each 'Witch Pricker' was paid per
convicted witch the whole exercise was extremely suspect.

Many people unknowingly still employ anti-witch charms to
protect themselves and their families, the most common being
the nailing of an iron horseshoe over an entrance door. It is not
the horseshoe which is lucky but that it is made from iron, and
almost since the Iron Age it has been believed that witches and
evil spirits will not pass under, over or through iron.

There was a strongly held belief that most witches gained
their extraordinary powers by making a pact with the Devil
in return for their souls. The Devil usually appeared to them

in the shape of a small animal such as a cat, bird, mouse or mole, and in return for certain favours became the woman's servant for life. That animal became the witch's imp or familiar and did her evil work for her.

Ellen Garrison, a supposed witch from Upwell, was hounded in 1645 by a witch-finder working under the direction of the loathsome Matthew Hopkins, the Witchfinder General. She was alleged to have been a witch for many years, as had her mother before her, and she had quarrelled with her neighbours and caused them to be ill on many occasions. Hopkins' accomplices told the Ely justices that they had watched Garrison in her house at Upwell, where they had seen an insect which looked like a giant beetle. The creature scuttled all around the room and under the woman's chair. It moved so fast it was in their opinion a familiar.

All familiars were supposed to live on their mistress's body and suck her blood which they took from a third nipple, which could be any protrusion from her body. Such a lump or ganglion was sufficient to condemn many reclusive spinsters who lived alone with their pets and were disliked by their neighbours. A common method for drawing a spell from the bewitched was to scratch the person who was believed to be responsible for the hex and who had sent her familiar into the body of her victim. As her blood began to flow the creature would rush out from its host to drink from his mistress. Imps had to be kept busy or else they were a terrible nuisance to their owner, who had to keep them under her armpit or tucked safely between her breasts. Some women were said to own seven or eight, which must have posed a problem when they were not working!

There was a further belief that a witch could not die until her imps were dead. One old woman was lingering between life and death and put her familiars into a red hot bread oven. They cried pitifully like newborn babies, but she remained steadfast and soon her wish was granted. Another woman similarly placed managed to get her nurse to take her imps for her. Their names were Bonnie, Cap, Red Cap, Jupiter and Venus and they were taken to Horseheath, where they were remembered in 1915. They were said to look a bit like mice, except that their eyes grew large and then returned to their normal size in a constant rhythm.

Within living memory some people, especially country folk, took great care to protect themselves and their families from the influence of witches. Besides nailing horseshoes over their doors, some would lay a steel knife under their doormats, for this metal had the same effect as iron. A jug of water would be placed in the chimney to stop her entering this way, for witches would not go near water and often rowan ash trees were planted close to cottages, with the same effect. It was further believed that in order to create evil the witch had to have something personal which belonged to her intended victim. Therefore mothers salted and burned their children's milk teeth, salt and fire being strong deterrents; all nail parings were burned, as were the gleanings taken from hair brushes and combs. Midwives always burned a woman's afterbirth for the same reason.

Witch balls, a corruption of 'watch balls', were hung in the front windows to avert the evil-eye. These coloured, mirrored glass balls came in a variety of sizes and look like large Christmas tree baubles. When a witch gazed into one it was supposed to bounce her stare away from the house and if one went cloudy it signified a witch was in the near vicinity.

If these precautions failed a common anti-hex practice was to take a small glass bottle which was filled with the victim's urine, pieces of hair (all personal objects to make the connection), some strands of red thread or wool to represent blood, shards of glass and about one ounce of new steel pins. The bottle was well stoppered and then placed carefully into a bright fire. The whole operation was done in complete silence. When the bottle burst the witch was said to feel a terrific pain shoot through her body. She would dash to her victim's home and beg for forgiveness and to take the bottle from the fire.

Silence still had to be maintained and if broken the witch's magic would live on, otherwise the witch removed the spell which in turn removed her pain. Sometimes a bottle with similar contents was placed in a wall as a general precaution. There is a very grisly looking witch's bottle to be seen in the Cambridge Folk Museum which still contains strands of hair. It was found in the tower of Swaffham Bulbeck church in the 19th century.

The witch with the best-sounding name has to be 'Daddy Witch' from Horseheath, who was a woman and remembered in 1915 as 'An ancient and bony creature, half clothed in rags, who lived in a hut by the sheep pound in Garret's Close, and gained much of her knowledge from a book called *The Devil's Plantation*.' When she was in her prime she frolicked with the 'Many wizards and witches who flocked around for miles around Horseheath and these frolics and dances were held at midnight in lonely fields by the master witch of the neighbourhood.' When Daddy Witch died, her body was buried at the crossroads close to the old sheep pound. Her grave was still marked in 1915 by the dryness of the road, said to be caused by the heat of her body, but modern road materials have now removed all traces of this strange woman.

Three of the most famous English witches are the 'Warboys Witches', Mr and Mrs John Samuel and their daughter Agnes, who were accused on 5th April 1593 of 'witch-murdering' Lady Cromwell of Hinchingbrook House, Huntingdon, the grandmother of Oliver Cromwell.

Warboys is an Old Huntingdonshire village situated on the rise above the North Cambridgeshire Fens. On 10th November 1589 Jane, daughter of Squire Robert and Mrs Throckmorton, went into a fit for no reason at all. The ten year old girl's limbs went stiff and jerked as if she had the palsy. Her eyes rolled and then she went into a deep trance. It was during one of these attacks that she accused old Mrs Samuel of being a witch though the old lady protested her innocence. Soon after this outburst the other four Throckmorton girls aged between nine and 15 years developed the same symptoms and made the same accusations whenever they saw Mrs Samuel. Then it was the turn of the Throckmorton's seven servants, who copied the girls. They were treated by two eminent Cambridge doctors, Barrow and Butler, who in the end were inclined to believe the witchcraft accusation as they could find nothing wrong with their patients.

In September 1590, Lady Cromwell visited the Throckmorton family and met Mrs Samuel whom she agreed was a witch. She snatched off Mrs Samuel's bonnet and cut off her hair, which she then burned to counteract her evil. The accused 'witch' cried 'Why do you treat me so, madam, for I have done nothing to you, yet.' After this altercation Lady Cromwell suffered from persistent nightmares, her health declined and she died in 1592.

Then the Throckmorton household's apparent mass hysteria changed course; mayhem broke out when they did not see Mrs Samuel, so she was forced to leave her own family and take up residence with the Throckmortons. The girls tormented her cruelly and scratched her without remorse. In December 1592 the old woman could take no more of their treatment and begged them to stop. They obeyed her immediately, which was interpreted as proof of her guilt.

She was handed over to the authorities, who stood her before the Bishop of Lincoln. After some 'encouragement' she confessed to owning eight familiars whom she had named Pluck, Harname, Catch, the three Smacs (all cousins), Blew and White. She was then carted off to Huntingdon gaol to await trial along with her husband and daughter, who by then had also been implicated. Various neighbours testified that they too had suffered the same illness as the Throckmorton household and that their cattle had died in strange circumstances. On 5th April 1593, Agnes Samuel, aged 80, her husband John and daughter Alice were found guilty of 'witch-murdering' Lady Cromwell and hanged the following day. Their bodies were stripped naked and left for public view.

During preparations for her burial, Mrs Samuel was discovered to have 'a little lump of flesh ... in the manner of a teat ... adjoining to so secret a place which was not decent to be seen'. Conclusive proof indeed that this humble, confused and tortured woman really was a witch.

For over 200 years the 'Witches of Warboys' were remembered in an annual sermon given in All Saints' church, Huntingdon each Lady Day. The sermons were paid for from the seizure of the Samuels' asscts, which had amounted to some £40, by the lord of the manor, Sir Henry Cromwell, husband of the deceased. This sum of money was paid to Queen's College, Cambridge to deliver the sermons, which did not stop until 1812.

William
The Reeve's Son

IN medieval times the Catholic Church was supreme and very wealthy, a combination which gave it great social and economic power. Most of the land in Cambridgeshire was owned by monasteries and it was from the manors of Melbourn and Meldreth, owned by the abbot of Ely, that young William, the reeve's son, held his 20 acres of land.

Within the manor the responsibilities of the lord of the manor's officials, stewards, bailiffs and reeves are recorded. In addition the status of his villeins, their services and other obligations and rents are all recorded in the Manor Rolls. These rolls were usually made from strips of vellum measuring between seven and twelve inches in width by 20 and 24 inches in length, stitched together to form long rolls.

A manorial survey undertaken in Melbourn in 1318 gives an elaborate list of the customary services required from its villeins. It is an interesting record of life in feudal England and is full of minutiae, stating when meals are to be taken, ex gratia payments to the prior (the lord of the manor), and who shall or shall not marry without the permission of the prior. The survey was made by two clerks and received the sworn testimony of eleven tenants.

To give an overall picture of the manor, its house enclosure contained over six acres and was with 'herbage and fruit from three gardens worth ten shillings per annum clear.' There was a windmill, a watermill and a dovecote plus 50 acres of enclosed meadow and a hop-ground. The arable land measured over 500 acres in pieces contained throughout the two parishes, and this was the demesne land only — land retained for the sole use of the prior. The other lands let out to tenants, which made up the 1,440 acres recorded in the Domesday Book, are not included in the survey.

A record of all the work to be undertaken by each villein is one of the most interesting sections of the document and the following is a condensed account of the services due from one man, William, the reeve's son. It records his messuage of 20 acres of land 'by the perch of 16 width' (one perch equals five and a half yards) for which he owes the following work:

'From Michaelmas to Christmas, every Monday and Friday in each week, if thrashing he shall thrash 24 sheaves of wheat, beans or peas or 30 sheaves of barley or dredge — mixed oats with corn, for a day's work and shall carry away the straw from such thrashing anywhere within the manor for another day's work. If carting or spreading dung, ditching, helping the thatcher, driving the plough or harrowing he shall work from rising to setting sun and it shall count as two works [two day's work]. If he only works until 3 o'clock it shall count only as one work, but he shall be allowed to go to his dinner at three o'clock without prejudice.

'He shall plough one acre of land for winter corn without allowance for work, or shall pay 4d. He shall make one perch of wall five feet high with foundation, two and a half feet deep. The lord shall supply the clay and hod, but he shall do his own carting. For all manorial work he shall supply his own tools except when winnowing his lord's corn.

'He shall carry four bushel [one bushel equals eight gallons dry measure] load of the lord's corn to Cambridge on Tuesdays, Thursdays and Saturdays, without allowances for work; if he shall be ordered to carry it on Monday, Wednesday or Friday he shall be allowed one work.'

From Cambridge, William and four other men bound to the estate had to take the corn in boats to Ely. On arrival each man received five black loaves [coarse bread], five measures of common beer, and either nine herrings, nine eggs, or two dishes of meat.

The document then sets out his services due from Christmas to Lady Day and then on to Lammas Day, the variations chiefly having reference to the sowing of spring corn and haymaking, with Easter Monday being a holiday. His harvest services were most important; from Lammas Day (1st August) to Michaelmas Day (29th September) he worked for the prior on Mondays, Wednesdays and Fridays, except on any Feast Days.

Amongst his other harvest services he had to find two men to work for the prior for four days' mowing and the prior was to reward each of them with three loaves of bread, six herrings, one halfpenny's worth of cheese, but no ale. He then had to provide two other men for four days' mowing who were to have the same quantity of bread and cheese and in addition a plate of meat each and as much ale as they wished to drink!

If the reeve's son had a stallion or bull for sale, if the prior so wished he was to be able to buy it at a fair market price.

William was not permitted to grind his corn at any mill other than the prior's, without a licence from him. He could marry his daughter to any of the homagers (men bound to the estate) without a licence, but not to a freeman without permission. His eldest son was to inherit, his other sons were not to live out of the town or to marry without licence. If he had no sons his eldest daughter was to inherit. After his death, the prior was to have his best beast as heriot (a death duty paid by a tenant to his lord) and the widow or next heir was quit of all services for 40 days thereafter. His widow was to have the holding for life, upon payment of a fine to the prior.

He also had to give a cockerel to the prior each Christmas, ten eggs at Easter and one penny on each Quarter Day. Should he be elected to the office of reeve he would be free of all service for his land for the time being.

William's obligations are a good example of the power of

the feudal system, whether the masters were ecclesiastical or secular. Each manor or monastic house was more or less a self-sufficient unit which jealously guarded its autonomy. The Manor Court was the central institution of medieval village life. 'Suit of court', the duty of attendance there, was one of the chief obligations of the tenants and was written into William's conditions. This central court supervised the organisation of the agrarian and social life of the manor.

During the 15th century the monks stopped farming the Melbourn and Meldreth estates, and let the manor on lease.

Dr Dodd's Malt Sermon

THE Reverend Doctor John Dodd (1549–1645) was a Fellow of Jesus College and although a staunch Royalist held extremely puritanical views. 'Old Dodd', as he was affectionately called by his contemporaries, made it his duty to expound on the evils of alcohol and made regular trips around the county on this mission. He particularly castigated the drinking habits of the collegians and was famous for his published *Sayings* such as, 'Brown Bread with the Gospel is good Fare.'

There are several versions of this strange sermon he is said to have preached, with two in manuscript form being in the British Museum.

One afternoon some students met Dr Dodd close to the village of Maddingley and decided to have some fun at the erudite teetotaller's expense. They implored him to give them a sermon on the Temperance question, there and then, and pushed him into a hollow tree which was to serve as his pulpit. His protests were made in vain and he was given the word 'Malt' for a text. Never being short of words, he gave the following sermon:

'Dearly beloved, let me crave your attention. I am a little man called upon to preach at a brief notice a short sermon from a short text to a small audience. My text is MALT. I cannot divide it into words it being one word only; I will therefore divide it into letters, thus M-A-L-T.

M — stands for Moral
A — for Allegorical
L — for Literal
T — for Theological.

The Moral set forth is to teach drunkards good manners, therefore:

M — Masters
A — All of you
L — Listen
T — To my text.

The Allegorical is when one thing is said and another is meant, the thing mentioned is MALT, the thing intended is the essential outcome of MALT which you make:

M — your Meat
A — your Apparel
L — your Liberty
T — your Trust

The Literal is according to the letter:

M — Much
A — Ale
L — Little
T — Thrift.

The Theological is according to the effects it works, these I find to be of two kinds: the first is in this world, and the second is in the world to come. The effects it works in this world are in some

M — Mischief
A — Adultery
L — Loose living
T — Tippling.

Secondly, in the world to come:

M — Misery
A — Anguish
L — Lamentation
T — Torment.

So much, then for this time and text. In conclusion I will give

83

you a word of admonition:

    M — Masters mine

    A — All of you

    L — Leave off

    T — Tippling.

Now for a word of commination:

    M — Masters

    A — All of you may otherwise

    L — Look for

    T — Troublesome times.

A drunkard is the despoiler of modesty, the annoyance of civilisation, the destroyer of nature and reason; he is the brewer's agent, the ale-house benefactor, his wife's sorrow, his children's trouble, his own shame, and his neighbour's scoff; a walking swill-tub, the picture of a beast and a monster of a man.'

Dr Dodd then bowed to his small but delighted audience and resumed his journey with great satisfaction.

The Cambridge Fish Book

THE two principal characters in this odd tale are John Frith, a 16th century Protestant reformist, and a large codfish stuffed with a religious treatise.

In 1626 a particularly fine catch of codfish was sent to Cambridge from the port at King's Lynn via the river Cam. It was delivered to a fish-woman's stall and she quickly set about gutting her stock to sell that day. Her nimble fingers pulled and sliced and she was nearing the end of her task when she noticed that the maw or stomach of a particularly fine fish was over-stuffed and hard. She applied her knife and pulled out a large slimy object wrapped in sailcloth. Carefully protected and in good order was a long forgotten volume of religious treatise by John Frith, none the worse for its seagoing passage.

After Frith had graduated from King's College, Cambridge in about 1527 he went up to Christchurch, Oxford where he wrote this rather unremarkable treatise on religious reform. He then went on to assist William Tyndale in Germany with his influential English translation of the New Testament. Both were accused of heresy as vernacular Bibles were at that time illegal in England, the church authorities maintaining they would allow the common people too much freedom of opinion. Upon his return to England in 1536 he

was seized and thrown into Oxford gaol, where he witnessed his companions one by one succumbing to its terrible conditions. Frith remained steadfast and in time was taken to London where he was burned at the stake on the charge of heresy.

The find of Frith's early treatise in the codfish caused quite a stir in Cambridge and soon word of it spread outside the area. Some local publishers reprinted the martyr's inspiring work, which was bought as much for curiosity's sake as for spiritual debate.

How the book ever came to be lodged inside the fish will remain a mystery. Did some sea traveller caught up in a raging storm wrap his treasured book so carefully in the hope of preserving his moral comfort? If a whale could swallow Jonah it should not be too difficult for a cod to swallow a small religious tract. Or was it the work of some Cambridge students who thought up this piscatorial prank which the gullible public swallowed hook, line and sinker?

A letter is said to be lodged in the British Museum, written by 'an educated man' who penned the following:

'I saw all with mine own eyes, the fish, the maw, the piece of sailcloth, the book, and observed all I have written. Only I saw not the opening of the fish, which not many did, being on the fish-woman's stall in the market, who first cut off his head, to which the maw was hanging, and, seeming much stuffed with something, it was searched and all found as aforesaid. He that had had his nose as near as I yester morning would have been persuaded there was no imposture here without witness. The fish came from Lynn.'

Waterways, Lightermen and Horse Knockers

EAST Anglia has a wonderful network of natural rivers, canals and drainage channels which, until trade was lost to the railways in the mid 19th century, was its main system of transportation. In Cambridgeshire materials were delivered in this fashion to build the beautiful Cambridge colleges and the county's fine churches and monastic buildings, including its jewels, the Ely and Peterborough cathedrals.

The Romans built several waterways including the Car Dyke, the straight rodden from Outwell to March and the Ouse channel from Prickwillow to Brandon Creek (Suffolk). They also built canals or lodes at Burwell, Reach, Bottisham and Swaffham Bulbeck which linked these villages with the river Granta (now the Cam). Throughout the Middle Ages monasteries undertook various drainage schemes, mainly to protect their own land, the most notable being the straight channel from Peterborough to Guyhirn which took the river Nene quickly out into the Wash via Wisbech. This cut known as Morton's Leam was initiated by Bishop Morton in 1478, completed in 1490 and is still in use.

However, the golden age really started in the early 17th century when Francis, 4th Duke of Bedford and his 13 fellow business adventurers put up the money to drain what is known as the Bedford Level. Sir Cornelius Vermuyden, the brilliant Dutch drainage engineer, devised the scheme which speeded the flow of the upland rivers out to sea by digging straight channels to bypass the sluggish natural bends. This prevented swollen rivers discharging onto the low lands and it also gave us some splendid water routes.

Since Roman times the main craft to use the waterways were barges known as lighters or fen-lighters, the design of which had changed little. These flat-bottomed boats were mainly built of oak or elm measuring some 40 ft long by ten ft wide with a load-bearing capacity of 25 tons. When empty they could float in just two feet of water and when fully laden only needed four feet. The main building yards were at Burwell, Cambridge, Isleham, Upwell, Ely and St Ives (Old Huntingdonshire).

The craft were usually worked in gangs of six, linked together with an ingenious system of spars or 'jarming poles', fastened with ropes and chains. It only needed two men to work the lot, plus a strong horse to tow the gang and a horseman or 'horse knocker' boy to lead the animal. The latter were often very young children, hired on the cheap with less value than the horse.

On a good day the gang could cover 20 miles but when they had to go through numerous locks or staunches this slowed them down to perhaps three miles a day. In very dry weather the crew had to make a temporary staunch to float the craft over very shallow water. This was done by sinking the horse boat and extending tarpaulins to hold up enough water to get the gang moving.

The leading craft was the lighterhouse with its ten to 15 ft high mast on which a square-shaped sail was hoisted in favourable weather conditions. The men slept and cooked in the lighterhouse, the home of the large pickle tub with its lumps of salt beef and pork. The gentle motion of the inland waterways was supposed to work the salt slowly and evenly into the meat, which produced a fresher tasting meal. This was much better, so it was thought, than the meat which heaved and sloshed around the tubs belonging to the seafaring traffic.

Life was not easy for the men, boys or horses. Most bridges which spanned the waterways were low, so the mast had to be lowered each time they had to go under one of these nuisances. There was rarely room for the horse to walk under bridges so this meant getting the quanting pole out and pushing the gang along. A man stood on the front bow, dropped the pole in the water and then walked aft using his weight to pull the boats along. When the tow path changed sides, the horse had to be swum across with the horse knocker standing on its back to keep himself dry.

The tidal stretch at Denver Sluice leading to King's Lynn involved long waits for a favourable tide. They also had to take a skilled berthsman or pilot on board to pass them through the tideway. Sometimes they could not get under bridges even with the mast lowered when spring tides raised the water level, so again they had to wait for the tide to turn. Most of this waiting was done in one of the scores of public houses which lined the haling way. Alcohol was banned from being taken on board but most employers gave their crew a beer allowance. The men were notorious drinkers and landlords chalked all allowances on a blackboard with the men's names and alongside their number of P's and Q's, or pints and quarters. It really was a case of watching your P's and Q's, as any excess had to be paid for by the drinker.

Cargo included fertilisers, building and road materials, coal, peat, sedge, sugar beet, grain, vegetables, fruit and passengers. Especially the latter on market or fair days. Most towns had their own dock or landing stage, otherwise everything had to be manhandled up and over the often steep river banks.

Tolls were collected at toll bridges and calculated on individual loads, eg in 1894 tolls on the river Cam included wheat and barley at 6d a score, timber slates and tiles at 3d per ton and sedge at 1d per ton.

The haling way or tow path was constantly churned up by the horses and their knockers or men, so in baking hot or freezing cold weather the tracks were turned into ankle-twisting obstacle courses. This must have been especially hard on the legs and feet of the small boys, some going barefoot in all weathers.

Animals were grazed along the river banks and fences were put up to the water's edge to stop them from straying. As there were no gates there was no way round other than jumping over and these fences were known as 'jumps'. There was real skill in getting the horse over. First the gang had to come alongside to allow some slack in the haling rope, at the right time the horse knocker thwacked his animal's rear end with his stick, shouted the appropriate words and the animal took a running jump and cleared the obstacle. These fences were supposed to be no higher than three ft but this was not always the case. There must have been some nasty accidents before a novice horse got the hang of jumping whilst still attached to a towing rope and a gang of barges.

The old time lightermen were said to be a strange breed of characters. Some were master poachers and thieves, the land-lord of the Jennings Arms at Denver Sluice having to chain his poker to the fire hearth to stop it wandering off. Their dress was flamboyant with sleeved waistcoats made from bright blue or red velvet, with tiny glass buttons. With their fustian or corduroy trousers and fur hats they must have dazzled any pub with their laughter and language as ripe as a pear in September.

The water trade had a tremendous boost when steam-driven beam engines were installed in the water drainage pumping stations. Upware was the first Cambridgeshire pump to have such an engine, which was installed in 1821 for the Swaffham and Bottisham Drainage Board. Soon most of the windmills were replaced by the steam engines; all requiring coal which was more conveniently delivered by lighters.

The Eastern Counties Railway Company laid the first railway in Cambridgeshire in 1845 when the main line from London to Norwich crossed the county. A line from Ely to

Peterborough was opened the following year and during 1847 several other lines were established. The water trade was slowly lost to the railways, which were cheaper and more convenient.

Trade was revived in the 1860s when coprolite or petrified dung was discovered in many parts of the south and south-east of the county. This made excellent artificial manure and much was taken by water to the fertiliser processing factories which were built during the coprolite 'rush'.

However, by the beginning of the 20th century the fertiliser trade had almost come to an end and by then the watercraft were taking on a new appearance. Steam was replacing the sail and horse, the old timers' bright clothes were rarely taken out of the cupboard and road transportation was posing a new threat. Loss of toll revenue resulted in many stretches of water receiving little maintenance and in time they became almost unnavigable. As time passed motor engines replaced the steam, trade took another dive in the 1940s, but sugar beet was still being taken to the sugar factory via Burwell Lode until 1963.

Now pleasure craft sail on the waterways and most of the public houses, so beloved of the lightermen, have been turned into valuable riverside houses or holiday homes. All the slates have been wiped clean and only the doors are chained.

The Power
of the
Toad's Bone

I N the time when horses were the major power in agriculture, both the animals and those who worked with and
looked after them played a vital role within the farm economy.
A good horseman was rarely without work for his skills went
beyond handling a team of plough horses, but extended to
attending them at times of illness, and more important, keeping them in top condition. All their special receipts or recipes
were written down in small pocket books which horsemen
kept with them at all times for they were a secretive and
suspicious group and reluctant to pass on their knowledge to a
third party. Many stipulated that their books be buried
alongside them in the churchyard.

Few horsemen would buy all their ingredients from one
source in case the chemist or shopkeeper should guess what
they were up to. Instead they would purchase one ingredient
from one source, a couple from another and so on.

One particularly interesting custom undertaken in this
county by some horsemen was the 'toad's bone', which was
supposed to give them complete mastery over all horses — at
a price. For in return for this fantastic skill they sold their soul
to the Devil. There are still many old horsemen who say that
although they were never 'toad men' they knew people who

were, and a few laugh at the custom which may now appear to be little more than an outmoded rural superstition. The practice should be treated with respect, for those who indulged believed implicitly in both the effectiveness of the ritual and the power of the bone. They were also ever aware of the dreadful price they had to pay, for each soul was collected by the Devil himself at the time of death.

The first part of the ritual was the killing of a natterjack toad, sometimes called the walking toad for it was supposed to stalk the countryside on its hindlegs. The killing took place at midnight under a full moon. The creature was then either buried in an ant heap or placed on a thorn bush where it remained until its bones were picked clean. Midnight at the time of the next full moon signalled the time for the last part of the ritual when the horseman gathered the toad's bone and made his pact with the Devil.

The skeleton was cast into a stream, whereupon the man had to follow it without losing his concentration for a split second or the whole procedure would be rendered ineffective. In time the breast bone broke away and floated in the other direction. This was the precious toad's bone which was quickly grabbed from the water and taken home. Some horsemen agree with the man from Burrough Green, near the Suffolk border, 'that it was a terrible ordeal for fierce contrary winds sprung upon a still night, strange sounds were heard and strange sights seen.' Others believe this was the work of the Devil who was present, testing the resolution of his next victim.

The man was now a fully fledged 'toad man', a person reborn from his surrogate human sacrifice, the small natterjack toad. He was no longer an ordinary mortal but a child of the Devil. Even now some horsemen are a bit cagey when asked about the toad's bone, as if even talking about it is not quite right.

Some men simply kept the bone in their pocket, others

soaked it, whole or powdered, in certain oils and substances which would either jade or call the horse. The horse has an acute sense of smell and can detect odours which are not apparent to humans. Some smells have the power to jade or stop the animal, other enticing smells can draw or call it. It would react accordingly with or without the help of an animal's bone, but the belief in the ritual and the ultimate debt made the bone almost magic.

Tales are told of men who could throw the gears (reins) of a big farm horse over a two-tined fork which had been pitched into a dung heap. The animal would be ordered to step forward and knock the fork over, but it would refuse to do so. It would stand completely motionless, as if bewitched, until its keeper told it to move. What probably happened was the man had rubbed some repulsive substance over the horse's fetlocks which revolted the animal but was not noticeable to its audience. When it was time to end the act the man would rub on some antidote by patting the fetlocks in a friendly fashion, but not before performing some extravagant gesture such as tapping on its hoof, one! two! three! saying, 'There, he'll do it now!'

Jading substances would sometimes be used by men who bore grudges towards their fellows or their masters past and present. They had the power to stop a horse dead in its tracks and leave it there all day, no matter how much the poor creature was cursed, beaten or pulled. The 'spell' could only be lifted by the person who had cast it for only he knew the antidote. Often a disgruntled man would place a rat or stoat liver in the bottom of a horse's food container, the smell of which is loathsome to the animal, who would refuse to eat although almost on the point of starvation.

The use of drawing or calling oils had similar miraculous effects, especially when a badly behaved or unbroken horse could be calmed down in an astonishing way and made to follow the horseman through the field gate and into the stable.

95

Aniseed, rosemary, thyme, laudanum, orris-root powder and especially oil of rhodium were just a few of the things which could calm a horse. Horsemen often sprinkled a few drops of rhodium on their coat collar each day for drawing power. Others preferred to use small 'sweating cakes' which were made simply by mixing flour and water to a medium consistency and baking in a slow oven. The cooled cake was then sweated under the right armpit for a week — never removed. The man then stood in the wind with the pungent cake crumbled in his hands. The horse would soon smell this delicious odour and come to the owner who had baked and worn the tasty morsel, which before being given to the animal to eat was first rubbed all over its nostrils into which the horseman then blew and spat ensuring that this particular animal thoroughly recognised the smell of its keeper.

If certain smells could work so efficiently on the behaviour of horses one wonders why men went through the ritual of the toad's bone? It has been suggested that this one act is a relic of the old secret trade guild called 'The Society of the Horseman's Word' which within living memory flourished in parts of Great Britain, especially in Scotland. Nothing appears to have been recorded that such a guild existed in East Anglia, but then it *was* secret! The 'Horseman's Word' is said to have held awesome initiation rites in which the apprentice was blindfolded and led through life-threatening ordeals in which he entrusted his very existence to the hands and discretion of his elders. The midnight toad practice was once perhaps witnessed by the members of the guild, which confirmed the rebirth of the initiate when he killed and claimed the toad. If this hypothesis is correct then the devil who claimed the soul was not the ruler of hell but the devil or chief of the guild, similar to the devil of witches' covens. Indeed the 'toad men' were often called 'toad witches'.

The men believed so fervently in their ritual that they could often no longer live with the knowledge of what they had done and the payment they had agreed. Some men dug a deep hole and buried the bone in the hope of rescinding their hellish debt. Others were said to go mad, for the devil strikes a hard bargain, especially with a lone person, at midnight, under a full moon.

Matters of
Life and Death

THE mystery and importance surrounding the beginning and ending of life has perpetuated superstition and ritual since time began. Most of the following are general folk beliefs and are certainly not exclusive to this county. However, many have been practised well into this century and some superstitions are still held to be true, or at least treated with some respect.

Life started a little too soon for those conceived out of wedlock. Thomas Wale from Shelford kept an interesting note book, which was published by his grandson in 1883 entitled *My Grandfather's Pocket Book*. Under the date of 24th October 1780 he copied out a printed address from the minister of Girton parish church.

'TO THE YOUNG WOMEN OF GIRTON PARISH.
Mr P, having observed with great concern that many of the young women of this parish when they come to be married, are already big with child, and wishing to put a stop to a practice offensive to decency, morality, and often destructive to their own happiness, does hereby promise to every young woman of sober behaviour belonging to the Parish who shall hereafter be married in this church while under the age of 25 years that he will, upon the birth of her first child (if that shall happen nine months after the day of the marriage) give her 10s for ye Christmas Dinner and also a

silver plate of 10s value, to be worn upon the breast each Sunday when she comes to Church, with this inscription, THE REWARD OF CHASTITY.'

Babies born at midnight or in the 'chime hours' of twelve o'clock, three o'clock, six o'clock and nine o'clock, had the power to see ghosts and spirits invisible to others. May 1st was a very unlucky birthdate and mothers expecting a child on this date would often lift heavy objects and jump up and down a week beforehand in the hope of inducing an early birth. If unsuccessful they would dose themselves heavily on poppy tea in the hope of stupefying their bodies and delaying labour.

A child conceived during a thunderstorm would always be strong and healthy with the powers of leadership, but many Northern Fen mothers refused to suckle their babies during a thunderstorm in fear that their milk might be contaminated with sulphur and brimstone. Raspberry tea was taken every day once pregnancy was confirmed to ensure an easy labour.

Before the 1936 Midwives Act stipulated that all local authorities should provide the services of a qualified midwife for all home confinements, many countrywomen relied upon their mothers to attend the birth of their babies or else used the services of the local handywoman. Such women generally helped families at their time of need by sitting with the sick, laying out the dead and attending births. Their services were usually voluntary but a donation was always welcome. There was obviously no anaesthetic for the mother, just a drop of gin in a cup of tea. When the child was born many old wives would take it on its first journey, which was towards Heaven. This offered the baby a life of good fortune and was undertaken by standing on a chair with the child cradled in her arms.

It is still believed in the Northern Fens that anyone born with a caul (unruptured membrane) covering the head cannot be drowned as long as the caul is preserved. These were carefully placed between sheets of paper by the old wives at the time of delivery and handed to the mother. Many of these fine brown skins have been framed behind glass and hang in living rooms.

One should always press a coin into a baby's hand when visiting it for the first time although people from Glatton (Old Huntingdonshire) preferred to take an egg, a pinch of salt and a penny as their suitable gift.

Some old wives did a little fortune telling after the birth of a woman's first child to divine how many subsequent children she was likely to bear. This was done by burning the placenta and however many pops and squeaks it gave off, this was the number of future births. It must have been distressing for a woman who had just undergone a long and painful labour to have to lie in bed listening to the hissing and popping emanating from the fireplace. The thought may have crossed her mind that if only the Girton medallion so generously offered by Mr P could be given for post-marital chastity, how sweetly it would glisten on her Sunday breast!

Life and death were close allies during those old-fashioned home births, where a mother had probably not seen a doctor throughout her pregnancy. Death appears to have been less awesome in those days. Far more people died at home surrounded by their family and many people drew comfort in knowing that their friend the handywoman would lay them out 'when their time came.'

When a death occurred the superstitious opened every door and window to allow the soul to fly to Heaven, otherwise it might become trapped inside the house and the tormented spirit would haunt the family.

It was traditional until well into this century for the parson to be told immediately after a death had occurred so that the 'Passing Bell' could be tolled — one pull for a man, two for a woman and three for a child followed by as many as the age of the deceased. There was a saying which was firmly believed by the superstitious that if a bell 'Tolled for a she, it would toll for three', meaning that for every woman who died two more people would follow.

It was also customary in many villages for the 'Winding

101

Bell' to be tolled when the dead person was placed in their shroud. It would appear that the bell ringing was retained in country areas longer than in towns.

Another very important ritual performed by families who kept bees was to go to the hives and announce any death or great unhappiness within the family. To omit this announcement would possibly result in the bees swarming, for they were supposed to sense sorrow and leave it unless they knew the cause. Some beekeepers would 'Tang' the bees by banging a tin tray with a stick as they made their way to the hive. Others gave the bees a little sugared beer to make them drowsy whilst other hives were decorated outside with black crepe as their own mark of respect to the deceased. Some old bee keepers in the Northern Fens still talk to their bees in times of great family stress.

Most bodies were kept at home before burial, the open coffin being propped up on a couple of chairs in the living room. It was customary for all friends and relations to visit the corpse to pay their last respects and touch or kiss it for good luck. A pile of salt was often placed on its stomach which was supposed to stop bloating. This was actually the survival of an ancient custom to ward off evil spirits. The salt was not wasted but kept for applying to itching chilblains and was considered to be the very best cure for this painful winter ailment.

A truly terrible sounding cure for tumours was told to the writer by Mr Reg Lambeth from Fulbourn, who was quite an expert on local folklore. He mentioned 'The Dead Man's Hand' which had been applied to a woman in the south of the county during his childhood. The patient had to lie alongside the dead body for the whole night with its hand on the afflicted part. True believers would expect to be healed in the course of the next few weeks.

The old coffin makers took a real pride in their craft and Mr Frank Allen, retired wheelwright, carpenter and coffin maker from Witchford explained how his wife lined children's coffins with thick white satin, edged with deep lace frills. There was a custom during his early working life of delaying the burial of an unbaptised baby until the burial of the next village woman. The tiny coffin waited patiently for its moment when it was placed at the foot of the woman's grave so that she could take the baby up to Heaven with her.

There was an incorrect belief that if a coffin was carried over private land this pathway would remain a right of way. If pins were stuck into every gate post en route the land would remain private. This belief probably stems from Roman times when no landowner could forbid access to any graves which lay within his property, as the graves were not part of the purchase. A coffin route existed between Great Paxton and Abbotsley (Old Huntingdonshire) until the last century. Known as the Bier Balk, it entered Great Paxton church by the now blocked north door.

There were many death omens, most of which were perhaps more important to rural folk than to their urban fellows. Many are still half believed by elderly people. Therefore beware of a clock that suddenly stops, a bird that taps on your window or a pigeon that sits on your roof. All signal death! Watch out for a falling picture, or a badly folded linen cloth which produces a diamond shape in its crease. Dread ever hearing the ticking spider which gets behind your wallpaper or seeing a coffin-shaped piece of soot hanging from your chimney. A blazing fire with one black coal in its middle, known as a 'fire hole' is another portent of death.

A farmworker from Christchurch strongly advised the writer to look out for the following three danger signals, any one of which has the power to cause instant death. The good news is that the first two are rarely seen and he was quite adamant that the third did not exist — that is a dead donkey, an out of work parson and a contented farmer!

103

The
Parson Drove
Woad Mill

THE Northern Fenland village of Parson Drove had the last working woad mill, which stood at Church End. It was closed around 1914 when it was sold to the Isle of Ely County Council and divided into smallholdings. Woad Mill Farm stands opposite the old church.

Woad (*Isatis Tinctoria*) was described by Gerard, the celebrated Elizabethan herbalist in his *Herbal*: It 'hath long leaves of a blewish green colour. The stalk growes two cubits [three ft] high, set about with a great number of such leaves as come up first, but smaller, branching it selfe at the top into many little twigs whereupon do grow many small yellow floures; which being past, the seed comes forth like little blackish tongues. They floure from June to September.'

He goes on to say that 'Caesar of the French warres said that all the Brittons do colour themselves with woad, which giveth a blew colour; which thing also Pliny doth testifie; In France they call it Glastum . . . wherewith the Brittish wives and their daughters are coloured all over and go naked in some kinde of sacrifices . . .'

Gerard ends his description, 'It serveth well to dye and colour cloath, profitable to some few, and hurtfull to many.'

The mill was indeed used for dye-making purposes, but by the turn of the 20th century woad was being displaced by more convenient synthetic colourings and it was mainly used for dyeing uniforms. It certainly was a profitable crop. In 1900 it sold at £20 a ton and one acre could yield up to 3 tons. It needed deep soil on rich new land, ideally recently ploughed pasture. This was often hired for three or four years with permission to harrow it and plant woad.

The seed was sown in rows eight or nine inches apart, between March and May. It was a very labour intensive crop and robbed the land of most of its nutrients. The pasture land usually needed some twelve or 15 harrowings to remove the clods, the crop required two or three weedings. After harvesting the root was left in the ground for a second crop that year. The leaves were picked when the plants were about eight inches high, the work mainly being done by women and children, who also did the weeding. The leaves were put into large willow baskets and sent off to the mill for processing.

This building was constructed to a traditional design with its walls made of sods of turf some three ft thick at the base, which narrowed towards the top. The turf was laid in a herring-bone fashion and the cone-shaped roof was constructed from timber and hurdles, with a reed thatch.

The three large conical grinding wheels were in the centre of the mill with a walk-way for the horse to plod round and round, turning the insatiable, heavy wheels. The leaves were tipped into the hollow centre where they were ground to a pulp. The mixture was then hand fashioned into balls about five inches in diameter, by men known as 'Woadmen' or more commonly 'Waddies', who placed them upon large trays which they balanced on their heads, on top of their special top hats, and took them off to the drying sheds.

Apparently you could easily recognise a 'Waddy' from his purple neck and hands. Transporting the balls to the drying sheds was a messy business as the juice seeped out and oozed all over the carrier.

The tall, open-sided drying sheds were clustered all round the mill and were crudely made from poles and hurdles, with wooden flat roofs. The balls were laid on shelves made of woven hazel and known as 'fleaks'. Each drying shed would usually have seven fleaks on top of each other and there the pulped mixture would remain until it had shrunk to the size of a small orange.

It was then taken to the 'couching sheds' where it was broken up into small pieces, laid on the floor and sprinkled with water and left to ferment, with more water being added when necessary. It took between 20 and 40 days for fermentation to be complete, depending on the temperature. At this stage of the process the woad gave off the most terrible smell, which has been likened to part-way between a badly managed stable and a cesspit. We are told that in 1492 an order was made, 'That no dryer shall henceforth put or throw the "Wodewater" in the lord's stream before 8 o'clock at night under pain of 40d per time' — which was a huge fine. Queen Elizabeth I is reputed to have so disliked this smell that she issued a proclamation that she did not wish to be driven out of the towns in which she was staying by the woad infecting the air.

When this smelly process had ended, the woad now resembled the texture of dark clay and was packed tightly into casks and sent off to the Lancashire and Yorkshire cloth manufacturers. Once it was correctly packed it would keep for years, even improving with age.

Mr Fitzallen Howard of Holyrood House, Spalding, Lincolnshire was the last owner of the Parson Drove woad mill.

Opium Eating
in the Fens

UNTIL the 20th century many people who lived in the low
lying, damp Fen areas of Cambridgeshire, in common
with similar people in the neighbouring counties, took opiates
as a form of self-medication and a means of dulling their
senses against the drudgery of living in such a wet, disease-
ridden environment.

This practice was centuries old before the 19th century
boom in the opium trade. Before that time they relied on
opium poppies to make poppy tea and poppy syrups. Most
gardens had a patch for growing the white and sometimes
blue *Papaver Somniferum*, which also grew wild. Some fields
were especially cultivated for the London market and the
flowers still crop up each year in some old, undisturbed
gardens. Farm labourers would take a bottle of the cold tea
with them into the fields for their 'dockey' or morning break,
which probably stupefied them for the rest of the day!

Doctor Charles Lucas worked in the Soham, Isleham and
Burwell fen areas of East Cambridgeshire and wrote in his
Memories of a Fenland Physician dated 1930: 'I do think this
(poppyhead tea) was the cause of the feeble-minded and
idiotic people frequently met with in the Fens. I have known
people of this calibre, when they wanted to go to the shop, put
one or two children into an empty brewing copper, give them
a piece of bread, then put on the lid, and there the children

would remain until their considerate parents returned, perhaps late in the afternoon.'

Until the 1868 Pharmacy Act made it more difficult to sell opium without a licence, it could be bought from any shop in any town or village and was even hawked by pedlars from door to door. Such people as grocers, drapers, boot menders, ironmongers and bakers, in addition to chemist's shops, all sold laudanum, a tincture of opium known as Godfrey's Cordial, opium pills and little penny sticks. The 1868 Act did not really curtail supplies to the Fens and it was the very chemists trading in these areas who were instrumental in getting opium removed from rigid control in Part One of the schedule, stating that if it was included they would suffer great financial hardship, as opium was one of the mainstays of their trade. They dispensed their own supplies of Godfrey's Cordial and in the 1800s many kept stocks of 40 gallons at a time.

Therefore there were always plentiful supplies throughout that century to feed the widespread addiction of the people who lived in the wetlands which stretched throughout the Isle of Ely, with its market towns of Wisbech, March, Chatteris, Littleport and Ely and all its many villages and isolated hamlets and droves. The east of the county had similar damp and addicted areas, which then swept over to the west as far as St Ives (Old Huntingdonshire) and Whittlesey in the north-west of Cambridgeshire.

Conditions started to improve during the last quarter of the 19th century, when life was still harsh but at least better than previous years when the ague, a type of malaria, was endemic throughout these areas. Quinine would have been an ideal relief for this painful and debilitating disease, but the price of just one ounce was equivalent to the cost of one pound of opium. Fen ague, rheumatism and poverty were said to be the three scourges of the Fens.

Until the 20th century medical services were sparse and centred on a few towns, which to poorly paid farm labourers living in the remote outlying Fens, might as well have been a thousand miles away when it came to making an emergency journey to visit the doctor. During bad weather the tracks and droves would have been turned into deep cart-rucked quagmires, denying access to both patient and doctor. Perhaps the main disincentive to seeking medical attention was poverty, considering the fee of two shillings and sixpence which would have had to be found from an average wage packet of between 18 shillings and 25 shillings, as late as the beginning of this century. Therefore most people had no choice other than to rely on their 'simples' or home cures, which often included the ubiquitous opium.

Opiates were not just confined to humans, but were given to animals as home remedies against illness and to keep them quiet so they would fatten more quickly. As one farmer observed, 'Pigs gits fatter quicker when they don't cry.' Unscrupulous horse dealers would give the drug to vicious horses before they were offered for sale. As late as 1924 the Home Office was concerned with the number of permits issued under the 1920 Dangerous Drugs Act to farmers in East Anglia applying for veterinary laudanum.

Opium eating in the 19th century can be equated with the analgesics and tranquillisers of our age. Laudanum was very popular with women for easing their 'nerves' and 'women's troubles'. High doses would be taken on 30th April if a pregnant woman thought she was likely to give birth on the following day, for 1st May was considered by the superstitious to be the most unlucky of all birth days. A strong dose of laudanum would render her comatose and stop contractions. Lethal doses were often given to illegitimate and deformed babies and sometimes one of a set of twins. Opium was used to ease toothache and neuralgia, rheumatism, diarrhoea, hangovers, headaches, gout, in fact it was the ubiquitous cure-all for any problem. Beer with an opium pill chaser was a favourite drink amongst the Fen men and much of the population was addicted from birth when they were given 'Mrs Winslow's Soothing Syrup' to keep them quiet and to soothe their teething problems.

One of the most sinister abuses of opium was that made by some women to keep their children in a semi-comatose state, with often tragic consequences. In the mid 1800s the itinerant system of farm labourers was introduced which took groups out to work on the large, under-populated acres of very fertile land which had been reclaimed by the recent drainage undertakings. Women formed a large part of the gangs, which kept them from home for most of the day. Some were lucky and were taken the required long distances by wagon, others less fortunate had to walk overall distances of anything up to twelve miles or more. They were forced to leave their young children at home, sometimes with an older sibling who would use the Godfrey's Cordial or 'Mrs Winslow's' with a free hand. Other mothers farmed their children out with dubious child-minders who also used the opium bottle with a heavy hand, especially in the case of hungry suckling babies. In the 1860s the infant mortality rate of 206 per 1,000 in small, rural Wisbech was higher than that of highly undustrialised Sheffield, with all its extra attendant problems.

In 1870 it was estimated that Fen-dwelling families were spending on average between eight pence and one shilling a week on 'opic', as they called it. Others spent far more. Thirty grains were equal to one pennyworth which was the dose taken by an habitual user, but hardened addicts could easily take 96 grains at one time. Suicide was not uncommon when people could no longer afford supplies.

Saturday was the traditional day for buying the next week's supplies for those who went to market regularly. Opium was easily obtained from the stall holders and from shops which stayed open late at night for that purpose. Some counters were piled with hundreds of small vials of laudanum. Charles Kingsley describes Saturday in Cambridge in his book, *Alton Locke*, published in 1850:

110

'Yow goo into druggist's shop o' market day, into Cambridge, and you'll see the little boxes, doozens and doozens, a'ready on the counter; and never a veneman's wife goo by, but what calls in for her pennard o'elevation, to last her out the week. Oh! ho! ho! Well, it keeps women-folk quiet, it do; and it's mortal good agin ago pains.
But what is it?
Opium, bo'r alive, opium!'

The Fens habit was little discussed outside the area and mainly condoned from within, many doctors being adamant that habitual use did not prevent longevity, neither was it damaging to health. The writer De Quincey observed in his *Confessions of an Opium Eater* in 1831 that the urban working class was using the drug as a cheap alternative to alcohol. The latter was considered to be a threat to lawful society, yet the rural habit was regarded as a good method for keeping an ague-ridden population docile and content. The alcoholic was supposed to say 'damn!' whereas the Fens opium eater said 'blessed.'

Nothing much was done about the situation until the formation of the Anglo-Oriental Society for the Suppression of the Opium Trade in 1874. This was largely a Quaker initiative and partly funded by the Pease family of Darlington. This led to a Royal Commission on Opium which sent representatives to the Indian sub-continent during 1893/94. But when its report was published it actually inclined on the side of opium.

However, over the ensuing years the Society gained more public support, led vigorous campaigns and lobbied Members of Parliament. This led to further legislation. Medical resources and standards of public health began to improve. Opium supplies were curtailed by the start of the First World War and all these factors, combined with the 1920 Dangerous Drugs Act helped to stop this ruinous practice by the end of the second decade of this century.

But the sad fact remains that during the 19th century

Wisbech was the town consuming the highest proportion of spirits and opium per capita throughout East Anglia and, as the *Morning Chronicle* reported regarding the 'Opium Eating City of Ely':

'You must make sewers to drain off the Godfrey's cordial and laudanum from chemist's shops.'

Elizabeth Woodcock's Dreadful Experience

THE winter of 1799 was very harsh. On the 9th February
the *Cambridgeshire Independent Press and Chronicle* reported
many tragedies resulting from the severe weather. Rebecca
Freeman aged 60 froze to death on the road leading from
Ickleton to Chesterford, John Limmer the shepherd of Wood
Ditton froze to death on Newmarket Heath, Abraham Rooks
was found dead on the road near Little Abington and William
Benett died from exposure on the road near Hardwicke. The
article then concluded: 'An Impington woman named Woodcock has been missing since Saturday and is supposed to have
perished in the snow. She left Cambridge at about 6 o'clock
in the evening and notwithstanding a diligent search, her
body has not been found. The mail coaches have in many
places been entirely stopt by snow and the mails forwarded on
horseback.'

However, Elizabeth Woodcock was not dead but very much
alive. She was the wife of Farmer Daniel Woodcock who
farmed in Impington and like most farmers' wives she worked
alongside him tending the geese and fowls, making butter and
cheese and doing the hundred and one jobs expected of a
country woman. Each Saturday she rode on horseback to the
Cambridge market where surplus goods were sold and provi-
sions purchased for the coming week. After she had conducted
her business she usually met her friends for a few drinks in the
market and finished off in the Three Tuns in Castle Hill on

her homeward journey. Alcohol was Mrs Woodcock's one vice; she could drink any man under the table and her bottle was never far from reach.

Elizabeth was not deterred from making her customary Saturday journey although the bitterly cold, steel grey sky presaged snow on that fateful 2nd February, 1799. Wrapping herself up warmly she loaded the horse, presumably took a few nips from her bottle and set off on her three mile ride to market. Her day was the same as any other, goods were bought and sold, a long time was spent in the warming Market Place inns and she left her drinking companions at about six o'clock when she set off for Impington. She stopped off at the Three Tuns inn as usual then finally went on her way, a most contented woman.

By now the snow was falling heavily and as the horse plodded slowly along the barely discernible trackway, the storm worsened. Huge drifts were building up along the edges of the dykes, but merry Mrs Woodcock was not troubled. All was well until she was about half a mile from her farm, when the horse was startled by a meteor which flashed through the black snow-laden sky. The poor creature reared up on its hind legs, scattering the befuddled woman and her groceries into a heap on the ground.

The horse bolted off to its stable whilst Mrs Woodcock made several brave attempts to stand up. This was finally achieved and she staggered off towards home leaving her groceries where they had fallen. After a short while she fell, totally exhausted, onto the ground where she lay in a drunken slumber and was soon covered by a large snow drift whipped up by the cruel wind that blew over Impington Common.

When the horse arrived home without its rider the Woodcocks and their neighbours made an immediate search of the area, checking every drift and calling her name. They searched long into the night and for several days thereafter. Eventually sense told them that Elizabeth must be dead and they would have to wait patiently for the thaw to reveal yet another victim of the relentless winter.

Whilst her family and friends were sorrowing over her assumed death, Elizabeth Woodcock was seated very soberly in her icy prison, comforting herself with her snuff box. On the following morning at daybreak she noticed a tiny hole in the top of the drift and that a small bush had also been incarcerated alongside her. She ripped off a piece of her red flannel petticoat, tied it to a twig and hoisted her distress flag through the hole, confident that someone would notice it that day. This was not to happen as she had staggered onto a part of the common that lay some distance from the normal pathway. So there the sad woman sat all through the following week, till Sunday when Mr Muncey of Impington happened to pass by and saw her red flag. He raced to the village for help and soon Mrs Woodcock was dug out of the drift and placed in a wagon which took her home.

The Cambridge newspaper reported her miraculous escape in its 16th February edition, saying that when she was rescued 'her voice and pulse were as strong as in full health. Her legs appeared like those of a drowned person and a mortification had taken place in consequence of their being buried in the snow.'

When she was sufficiently recovered to answer questions she said that she had hardly slept at all throughout her ordeal, neither had she ever lost consciousness. She was totally aware at all times and had had nothing at all to eat except snow. After the first night her snuff box gave no further comfort as she had lost all sense of smell. The effect of the 'mortification' of her legs (frost-bite) was terrible and despite her immediate robust voice and pulse, she was a very sick woman and often on the brink of death.

In time her health did improve a little and she once again gained happiness from her snuff box and her stout. People called from miles away, some whom she had never met before, all to witness at first hand the woman who had survived such a long time in such terrible conditions. By this time word had spread that Mrs Woodcock liked her tipple and most visitors brought a bottle with them, despite her doctor's orders. So the alcoholic farmer's wife lay in bed, the centre of attraction with plenty of supplies hidden from view. Her health deteriorated and in July she died.

She was buried in Impington churchyard but no stone marks her grave. Her burial notice is in the parish register:

'On the eleventh day of July, 1799 Elizabeth Woodcock wife of Daniel Woodcock, aged 43 years of a lingering Disease in consequence of a confinement under the snow of nearly eight days and nights, that is to say from Saturday the second till Sunday ye tenth day of February 1799.'

Under this inscription someone has added:

'She was in a state of intoxication when she was lost. NB. Her death was accelerated (to say the least) by spirituous liquors afterwards taken — procured by the donations of numerous visitors.'

It is assumed that her husband and family moved from Impington as there are no further records relating to the Woodcock family.

A monument commemorating her ordeal was erected near to the spot, but was spoiled by the huge numbers of visitors who went to see it. It was replaced in 1849 with the existing inscribed marker which stands in a field on the Chivers estate.

The
Great Bridge
of
Bourn

❦

BOURN village clusters around the old Stump Cross to Newmarket turnpike road. This is close to where the main road from Cambridge to Colchester used to cross the London to Newmarket road. A tiny brook, fed from springs near Bartlow, flows through the settlement, eventually joining the river Cam between Stapleford and Shelford to the east.

The present rather dull looking bridge, bearing the incongruous inscription, 'The Great Bridge of Bourn', was built in 1950, replacing the old 1762 stone construction, the true claimant to the inscription, which in turn succeeded a low wooden platform near to where a once popular and health-giving mineral water was drawn from Jacob's Well. It is hard to date precisely when the well was stopped, but it was probably in the first quarter of the 18th century.

In the 18th century the bridge was the fashionable haunt of the local gentry and students from Cambridge University, who flocked to the elegant King's Arms inn which stood at the foot of the bridge. The White Hart and Harp inns opposite were used by the less elite. Bourn Bridge was also a major stopping point for the coaching trade and the two latter inns handled all the parcels for delivery and collection.

The King's Arms was built on an incline and so dominated the scene. Its rooms were of elegant proportion and there was a bowling green and well laid out gardens, along with 50 acres of arable and pasture land. Many of the clubs and societies attached to the University held their dinners and other social events at the inn. These parties often turned into rowdy drunken brawls — it was nothing to see staggering young men performing daring tricks on the parapet of the bridge for large wagers. One night a student was so drunk that his colleagues had to lock him up in a bedroom in fear that he might wreck the inn. The prisoner went straight to the window and jumped about 30 ft onto the ground below, dusted himself off and returned for more wine. He was offered a large sum of money to do it again, but after careful consideration declined the bet!

In the summer months large marquees were set up in the garden for the archery meetings, where delicate refreshments were served to the archers and their guests, followed in the evening by a dinner which lasted well into the next morning when they reeled out and into their coaches bound for Cambridge. The main truly magnificent diary event of the year was the County Ball, when hundreds of finely dressed people converged onto the bridge, to see and to be seen.

The justices met in the King's Arms to renew local victuallers' licences and rooms were hired for transacting business by the Commissioners for Land Tax for the division of Linton and Bottisham and by the trustees of the turnpike road.

The road tolls were collected on the bridge, at one time from the White Hart Inn and then in the 18th century from a little brick-built gatehouse close to the principal inn. The toll point was called the 'Bourn Bridge and Babraham Gates,' Babraham being a continuation of Bourn.

It must have been a glorious sight to see the horses being reined in as they came down the two hills which flank the bridge, pulling passenger coaches with such evocative names as the *Expedition* and the *Diligence*. By 1750 coaches were calling at the bridge at all hours throughout the week. The *Diligence* was advertised in 1779 as carrying three persons for a guinea-and-a-half each, starting from the White Hart, Fetter Lane, London for the King's Head, Norwich three times a week, calling at Bourn Bridge. Passengers were allowed 14 pounds of luggage free and all above that weight was charged three pence per pound extra.

In addition to the passenger trade, carrier carts plied their way to London, Swaffham and Thetford (Norfolk) and Bury (Suffolk) on a regular basis, with the bridge being an important collection and delivery point. The mail coaches bound for London, Norfolk and Suffolk also collected and delivered from the bridge and the King's Arms kept a livery of some 30 horses for private hire. A terrible tragedy happened early one morning in July 1790 when a fire broke out in the stable block. It raged so fiercely that before anyone could dash to the rescue, six horses belonging to the Norwich Mail Coach were killed and the entire stables razed to the ground.

With so many wealthy people and carriages offering valuable cargo passing over this area, there is small wonder that this was the haunt of highwaymen and footpads. In 1784 three masked 'men of the road' stopped and robbed several wagons bound for Stump Cross. Whipping up their horses they galloped off to Six Mile Bottom where this time they relieved several people of their cash and jewels, then as if without a care in the world they tied their horses to some trees close to the bridge, from where they caught a post chaise into oblivion.

Carrying the mail bag was always a dangerous occupation and in 1792 the boy in charge of the Ely and Cambridge letter bags destined for London was overcome by three burly strangers. He was viciously beaten and dragged off to the woods where he was bound, gagged and blindfolded. His assailants proceeded to remove all the valuables from the mail, said to be worth about £5,000, buried the evidence and took off leaving the poor boy to his misery. A reward of £200 was offered for the capture of the robbers, but they were never discovered.

Quite a stir was caused in 1779 when a member of the local gentry was assaulted one September evening just before dusk. The son of Colonel Adean of Babraham Hall was returning home on his horse and within sight of his home when a footpad rushed out from behind a tree. He was brandishing a pistol and tried to make a grab for the horse's bridle. The frightened, high spirited creature reared up on its hind legs and then took off like the wind with young Adean still mounted and despite several slugs being fired, both returned home unharmed. A reward of five guineas was offered for this masked man dressed in a blue or a dark coloured greatcoat and a slouched hat. One would think that more robbers would have been caught when such valuable rewards were offered, but most seem to have escaped scot free.

A little further up from the bridge is a spot known as 'Langden's Grave', where the bones of a notorious local highwayman, Geoffrey Langden, are said to rest. Rumour was that this Langden was an ancestor of Robert Langden, who until his death in 1777, kept the White Hart. He and his family vigorously denied this allegation, but their name came into disrepute once again when in 1776 the Customs and Excise men seized some £2,000 worth of tea and lace, hidden up in the dog kennels at the rear of the inn. These large buildings were used in season by packs of beagles and foxhounds which were hunted from the bridge.

In 1791 the doors of the White Hart closed forever and the house became the private residence of Mr Richard Christling.

The demise of the Bourn Bridge settlement came with the building of the railway, which changed the fortune of so many old traditions, by offering a quicker and more convenient form of transportation. For several years the King's Arms had been steadily losing trade to more fashionable inns and it was demolished in 1850.

Today it is hard to visualise the exciting, bustling times of the old hump-backed 'Great Bridge of Bourn,' when its surface was swished by fashionable skirts and highwaymen's boots. The Duke of Wellington inn has replaced the former gathering spot of the rich socialites and the cypress-lined gardens have given over to houses. Only the brook remains; it is very small, no larger than a ditch, but still it makes its determined journey to meet the river Cam.

Black Shuck
and
The Shug Monkey

BEWARE of the spectral dog! Watch out for this 'Hateful Thing', alias Black Shuck, the East Anglian dog-fiend who often strays into the Cambridgeshire Fens and Washlands. Take special care when walking alone at night, when your solitary imagination is easily fired by the blasting wind or scudding clouds which darken the moon. This is the time when you are most likely to sense the thundering yet silent pattering of footsteps, or hear the raucous blood-chilling baying of some unhallowed beast. Watch out for one or two sulphuric yellow eyes burning from some shadowed cover, for Black Shuck the Hound of Odin is abroad. Such a meeting presages death within a year, although many have lived to tell their tale. His master is none other than Odin, the Father of the Norse Gods and protector of slain heros who were brought to Valhalla by his servants the Valkyries.

This monster stalks across most of the isolated regions of East Anglia and has various names such as the Snarley Yow, the Galley Trot, Old Scarfe and to those too scared to speak its name it is called the 'Hateful Thing'. It has been suggested that its popular name Black Shuck comes from the Anglo-Saxon 'Scucca' or 'Sceocca', meaning Satan. Like the Hound of the Baskervilles,

it has its roots in Scandinavian mythology, having been brought to the region some thousand years ago by Viking raiders.

Reputed to be the size of a calf and as black as sin, it often sheds one eye so that it resembles Cyclops with its one remaining eye planted squarely in the middle of its forehead. On some occasions it is headless, yet still has the ability to move with the silence and the speed of a cheetah. Black Shuck can vanish without trace so you think your eyes have been playing tricks. Only your pounding heart and raised body hairs tell you that the hell-hound has been close by.

Throughout this century many people have reported seeing the black dog in places in Cambridgeshire, including the Northern Fens, the fens around Soham and Wicken, isolated spots around Ely and the Ouse Washes. As recently as the winter of 1988 a mother and her young son were walking towards Parson Drove along the Throckenholt road. They were proceeding quite happily when suddenly, for no apparent reason, they both felt ill at ease. They stopped dead in their tracks when they saw one enormous yellow eye staring at them from the cover of some dark bushes. After a little while the 'thing', said to be the size of a calf, crossed their path and vanished without trace. Later they were told they had come face to face with Black Shuck.

In West Wratting, which lies on the Cambridgeshire-Suffolk border, the 'Shug Monkey' once haunted a lonely and little-used lane known as Slough Hill. This was a turning off the West Wratting to Balsham road and a place where few children ventured after dark. The Shug Monkey was a cross with Black Shuck and like its fellow fiend, had Viking origins. Having the body of a large, black, shaggy-coated dog, it had the face of a monkey with huge, disconcertingly shining eyes. It sometimes shuffled about on its hind legs and other times preferred to go on all fours. The Shug Monkey appears to have gone away, having not been seen since before the Second World War.

It is not hard to understand the reason for people's belief in the strange and supernatural. Until well into this century many isolated Fen areas presented ghostly images when small flames of self-igniting marsh gas materialised into 'Jack o' Lanterns', being an evil in their own right. Before the days of mass home entertainment and easy travel, people enjoyed telling tales, especially during the winter when they had more time to spare from working on the land. Women enjoyed meeting for a cup of tea and a frightening yarn. As one elderly man said, 'Them littl' ol' gals jest loved to frit each other and then they'd run off home as quick as they could, scared to death in the dark!'

Improved drainage and subsequent cultivation has put a stop to Jack 'o Lanterns, yet there is still something intimidating about the lonely Fens, especially on dark nights when the 'Lazy Wind' is blowing. This is a very strong wind which cannot be bothered to blow round you but goes straight through you! Perhaps it is the hugeness of the sky and flat land which makes one feel very insignificant and vulnerable to any unusual sound or movement.

Most of us would consider ourselves far too worldly today to believe in Black Shuck or the Shug Monkey. But what about tonight, should we have to walk alone down a straight and endless Fen road with only the night creatures and a lazy wind for company?

Bibliography

The Pattern Under the Plough Ewart Evans (Faber and Faber)

Cambridgeshire Customs and Folklore Edith Porter (Routledge & Kegan Paul)

Popular Rhymes and Nursery Tales of England James Orchard Halliwell (Bodley Head)

The Encyclopedia of Witchcraft and Demonology R H Robbins (Spring Books)

Riotous Assemblies 1740–1822 Paul Muskett (Earo Ely)

Blood or Bread A J Peacock (Gollancz)

A History of Cambridgeshire Bruce Gallaway (Phillimore)

Fenland Notes and Queries Vols 1–X11

Lord Orford's Voyage Round the Fens in 1744 (Cambs Libraries Publication)

Fenland Lighters and Horse Knockers R H Cory (Earo Ely)

A History of the Fens J Wentworth Day (E P Publishing Ltd)

East Anglia Magazine September 1955

Hunts & Cambs Archeological Society Vols 1–1V

Opium in the Fens in the 19th century V Berridge (Offprint from the Journal of the History of Medicine and Allied Sciences Vol XXX1V No. 3)

Narcomania on Heroin Merek Kohn (Faber & Faber)

Magna Brittannia — Cambridge

Skating J M Heathcote and C G Tebbutt (Longmans Green & Co 1894)

The Skaters of the Fens Allan Bloom (Heffer)

Memories of a Fenland Physician Charles Lucas (Jarrold & Sons)

The Cambridgeshire Landscape Christopher Taylor (Hodder & Stoughton)

Cambridge Antiquarian Society Communications Vols 1–XV

The Victoria History of the County of Cambridgeshire and the Isle of Ely

The Canals of Eastern England J Boyes & R Russel (David & Charles)

The Cambridgeshire Coprolite Mining Rush Richard Grove (The Oleander Press)

Leaflets of Local Lore 'Urbs Camoritum' (Newton & Denn)

Cromwell our Chief of Men Antonia Fraser (Weidenfield & Nicholson)

The Witches of Warboys Moira Tatem (Cambridgeshire Libraries Publication 1993)